HILLFIRE
ANTHOLOGY

VOLUME FOUR

HILLFIRE PRESS

HILLFIRE ANTHOLOGY · VOLUME 4

Hillfire Press Ltd
33 Melbourne Place
EH39 4JS

Published in 2025

Copyright © Respective Authors, 2025, moral rights asserted.

Design and typesetting by Amos O'Connor
Cover illustration by Amos O'Connor

Typeset in Hightower and Iowan Old Style

Printed in the UK

ISBN: 978-1-7396226-3-3

hillfirepress.com

HILLFIRE PRESS

Editor-in-Chief
Lena Kraus

Executive Editor
Carly Craig

Art Director
Amos O'Connor

Social Media Managers
Miriam Huxley
Wren True

Financial Coordinator
Julia Guillermina

Workshop Coordinator
Wren True

Website Managers
Wester Wagenaar
Miriam Huxley

Blog Coordinators
Katie Hay-Molopo
Miriam Huxley

Event Managers
Laura de la Parra Fernández
Tess Simpson

Copy Editors
Carly Craig
Katie Hay-Molopo
Miriam Huxley

Editors
Gerry Stewart
Carly Craig
Hayley Bernier
Hanna-Maria Vester
Miriam Huxley
Katie Hay-Molopo
M. H. Monica
Nicole Christine Caratas
Wester Wagenaar
Wren True
Alexia Wdowski

Proofreaders
Carly Craig
Gerry Stewart
Alexia Wdowski
Katie Hay-Molopo
Nicole Christine Caratas
Lena Kraus
Hayley Bernier

Fundraising Coordinators
Julia Guillermina
Miriam Huxley

FOREWORD

Welcome to Volume Four of Hillfire Anthology!

Hillfire Press is based in Edinburgh, Scotland. Our name comes from the way bright gorse lights up the Edinburgh hills in spring. This year, the imagery of many little gorse flowers creating a powerful effect together is particularly poignant to me. In response to their governments' drift towards fascism, people have been coming together in peaceful protests at dusk, raising lanterns, candles, and their lit-up phones. These oceans of light ("Lichtermeere" in Germany, where I first came across this concept) are a powerful message of unity, democracy, and solidarity.

In bringing attention to language through stories and poems, I hope that Hillfire Press can play a small part in upholding these values. Language is a powerful tool with which to shape our reality. Dehumanising language and populist slogans lacking in nuance pave the way for fascist regimes and legislation. Whatever your cause, resorting to this kind of rhetoric will foster separation instead of unity, loneliness and confusion instead of community. In communicating with empathy, in storytelling, we reveal our shared humanity and create connection.

When I started Hillfire Press, I innocently thought that our sole purpose would be to support each other's writing and to publish our words. The last few years have made it clear that creating true communities and living in them as we want to live in the bigger context of society is a powerful form of hope and resistance. I am grateful to everybody who has been part of this.

I hope you check in on your friends and invite them over for soup today.

Thank you so much for supporting us by buying this book. Please tell people about us. I hope you enjoy the read.

Lena Kraus
Founder, Editor-in-Chief

A NOTE ON THIS BOOK

This book has been produced by writers from all over the world, which is reflected in different varieties of English.

We have included content identifiers in the table of contents, much like allergens on a menu. If there are topics you don't want to read about, we have hopefully provided you with a means to avoid them.

CONTENTS

Julia Guillermina	3	Silent Night
Ruby Vallis	9	The Red Stag*
Malina Shamsudin	14	Striking-up Smoke‡
Miriam Huxley	19	Manifesting
Emerson Rose Craig	27	Give Me My Greatest Desire
Wester Wagenaar	32	We Do Not Want Him†
Thomas Carroll	40	●
Tess Simpson	45	The Winter Class
Hanna-Maria Vester	51	A Sleep‡
Hanna-Maria Vester	54	Crowded
Alexia Wdowski	59	Invitation to the Wedding
M.H. Monica	64	Where the Flowers Fall*
Elena Sims	70	Application for Solvers of World Peace
Nicole Christine Caratas	73	Recipe for a Love Potion
Alex Penland	76	Erasure◊
Wendelin Law	78	They are eating the cats! They are eating the dogs!†‡
Gerry Stewart	82	In My Allotment of Blank Books, Tea, and Anticipation
Gerry Stewart	84	Marching Away
Gerry Stewart	86	haunted

Wren True	88	Picketts*
Hayley Bernier	93	everything is the outstretched hand
Hayley Bernier	96	You Do Not Have To Be Good
Hayley Bernier	98	Ask the River, Ask the Sky, Ask the Person Standing Next to You
Katie Hay-Molopo	100	Aftermath
Laura de la Parra Fernández	105	For the time being
Carly Craig	109	Last Snow in Athens

CONTENT IDENTIFIERS

Grief/Loss * Xenophobia †

Murder/Death ‡ Homophobia ◊

JULIA GUILLERMINA

Silent Night

It was getting dark outside, the time of the day when solitude comes crawling, but the lights were not yet on.

Sole was scrubbing the stove after eating alone in the kitchen, again. Quique had come home from the gym just as she'd started cooking. He'd said *¿Qué tal?* before disappearing into his room. Dusa had arrived afterwards, saying hi to no one in particular while leaving her coat on the hanger near the entrance. She'd spared a glance towards Soledad, who had answered, but had climbed upstairs to her room the next second.

Sole stopped scrubbing. The silence piled up in the house. And that top left burner still didn't work. It made the fuse trip when you switched it on. Sole had told her flatmates at least twice, but they rarely used the common kitchen, and the landlord was a nuisance anyway. She sighed, rinsing the soap, listening to the foam bubbles pop. Her hand stopped near the top left burner. What if she switched …? She looked at the entrance, calculating. It was no use. It was a bad idea. The staircase was four steps away, just past Quique's door. And then there were sixteen steps to the upper floor. She would not make it unseen.

She dropped the cloth in the sink. Quique was watching Spanish political commentary on his computer; Sole could hear their angry voices. And Dusa would be watching something as well. Solitude was there for them all.

Sole looked at the stove ... and her hand reached the switch for the top left burner.

She had to be quick, but she had to be quiet.

Quique's video was bound to be loaded and last for a minute or two without connection. Sole could climb the stairs before the noise in his room stopped. Dusa could hear, though. Her room was next to Sole's. If she were to get out, she would bump into Sole running to hide, and the cat would be out of the bag. And she was smart. Sole knew that, even if they didn't speak that much, English being the only language they had in common.

Sole could only count on the fact that Dusa was tired after a whole day of work, and she wouldn't want to leave her room, even without lights.

She swallowed, firmly gripping the burner's switch. On the count of three.

One.

Two.

Three.

She switched it on – the stove turned on and blacked out – then off and jumped to the carpeted floor beyond the kitchen. She strode the three steps to the bottom of the staircase and tiptoed as quickly as possible up the flight of stairs. When her left foot touched the landing, she reached for the doorknob of her room. She grabbed it, twisted, opened the door, hurtled into her room, and yanked the door shut.

Sole pushed the light switch, just to check. No lights. She rested against her door and let her body glide to the floor. There she sat, her back against her bedroom door. Her heart was pounding in her throat, and she didn't dare breathe, lest she do it too loudly. Taking small, ridiculous breaths, she put her ear to the door and waited. She could hear some rummaging in Dusa's room. Then nothing.

Were they going to react at all? She pulled her lower lip into her mouth, trying to cut a bit of dry skin with her teeth. Maybe her flatmates were the only humans capable of sitting quietly in a room alone without electricity.

Her hands touched the parquet flooring. She was thankful for it. Downstairs, Quique had transformed what was meant to be a living room into his bedroom, and he had carpet flooring. The joys of British renting. Sole preferred the clay floors of Andalusian houses, but wood was okay. Her teeth finally gripped the dry skin and pulled. The soft tissue ripped, and she cursed under her breath. She tasted the metallic flavour of blood on her tongue.

Suddenly, she heard a door opening and Quique's voice rising.

'Hey? There is someone?' he called, with his Spanish accent and Spanish phrasing.

Sole's heart jumped in her chest. It worked! She kept still as a statue, with her lower lip still in her mouth.

Dusa moved in her room. Her door – finally! – creaked open.

'Quique?' she said, probably from the threshold.

'Dusa?' he called back.

'What's the matter?' Dusa asked, getting closer to the staircase. Quique's heavy step thudded up the stairs.

'The light is gone.'

'Oh, I didn't notice,' she lied. She didn't fool Sole.

'Ah,' said Quique in Spanish. He didn't believe her either. 'Eh …' he started. 'Eh … Maybe you were using your heater?'

'No, I wasn't,' she snapped. Sole smiled at the drama unfolding. 'You've asked me to be careful. Look, I'm wearing three jumpers.' Dusa sounded defensive. She often said she would never get used to the Scottish cold, and it wasn't even winter. Sole had never imagined Slovakia as a warm place, it being north of Spain, but she figured she had to change her prejudices.

Sole was sure Quique had his I-don't-believe-you face on.

'You can come and see.' Dusa changed her tactic and moved to her bedroom door. Quique climbed up two steps, getting cold feet.

'I ...' he muttered.

'Look, Quique, come and see. It was really not on. Come and check,' Dusa insisted.

Quique wasn't climbing. He must be standing in the middle of the staircase, dumbfounded.

'No, Dusa, it's okay. I believe you. I believe you.'

For a moment, you could hear a pin drop. Sole tried to imagine their faces. Were they looking at each other, Quique so big and scary, Dusa so tired of everything? They were opposites, really. Dusa was fat and tiny, with tiny hands and a tiny nose on her round face. She wore comfortable clothes, which were covered by her white hospital lab coat when she went to work. Her brown hair was wavy. Her face was amiable. She looked like a mum. Quique was tall and muscular, with big hands made to lift weights. That was what he did all day when he wasn't serving coffee to passengers on the ScotRail trains: strength training and protein eating. He wore his hair close-cropped and had a low, guttural voice.

A step creaked, and Quique spoke again. 'It must be something.'

It was *someone*, Sole thought, but she wanted to stay hidden. Were they just standing there, dead quiet? Quique thinking Dusa had her heater on, no matter what she said, Dusa, tight-lipped, wishing she had had her heater on, because at least then she would have been less cold.

'Is Sole home?' Quique asked.

'Maybe she's gone? She would have come out.'

Quique finished climbing to knock at Sole's door. Sole, on the ground behind the door, panicked. She dragged herself to the wardrobe and stood in the small space behind the door.

'*Sole, ¿estás en casa?*' he asked. Sole resisted, mute as a mouse. 'Okay, she is not here.' Sole breathed again. 'Can we go down and look at the electric … the electric panel? Maybe it's the neighbourhood.'

Sole could imagine Quique speaking with his hands, making gestures as he always did when trying to make himself understood. Dusa spoke better English than him, but she was patient, trying to live in harmony with her flatmate. Quique used to tell Sole that it was better living with people who spoke your language because it made it easier when discussing the house.

'It's always tricky,' he would say in Spanish, discreetly pointing towards Dusa's room.

Sole, whose attitude in the flat was making herself invisible to avoid being asked to clean the bathroom again (she never cleaned the bathroom, but tried to compensate by scrubbing the kitchen with her heart and soul), openly agreed with him and secretly wondered if she could get away with more if Quique didn't speak Spanish.

Quique and Dusa went down the stairs to check the electrical panel. They would soon discover the fuses had tripped, and it would be the end of the show.

'Oh, the ... thing is down,' Quique said. Sole still heard him through the flooring. The walls were as thin as paper, which didn't help with heating either.

'Yeah,' Dusa answered.

'I think we can just put it up,' Quique commented.

Some words were lost to Sole, who was imagining them discussing the reason for the tripping. She would have preferred them to talk upstairs, where she could really hear them, close to her.

'Me too,' Dusa said distinctly.

'Eh ... good night.' Quique's deep voice was comforting.

'Good night to you too. Thank you.' She didn't need to thank him, but she was nice like that.

'No, nothing, nothing ...'

The door downstairs closed gently, and Sole heard Dusa trekking up the stairs.

It was dark outside and inside. Dusa closed her bedroom door.

The silence piled up in the house.

RUBY VALLIS

The Red Stag

The brushes, oil paints, solvent, and a water flask clanked in her rucksack at the rhythm of her steps. Isla hoped the palette knife wouldn't make a hole in the packed lunch the kitchen staff had prepared for her at the hotel. She walked up from the Wee Bookshop, wondering whether this was the right way. The slope didn't look familiar. It took her to a wild patch of land without a defined path, where brambles and stinging nettles punished her naked legs.

Out of breath, she rested. As she turned to face the sea, time seemed to stop; pink heather, ferns, and foxgloves around her sprang to life like ballet dancers. The water glittered. Diamonds rode crested and foamed waves. Her tongue tasted salt and seaweed. She remained still until the screeches of seagulls stirred her out of her reverie. They chased a fisherman's boat, returning with the day's catch, reminding her of her grandparents, who had also lived on this island and existed on the fruits of the sea until the day it swallowed them. Their boat and their bodies were never found. Isla was five when it happened. Her mama wouldn't speak about it, but she finally opened up after her last rounds of chemotherapy when she said, 'They were called Angus and Ailsa. He came from a line of fishermen, and Ailsa was a foundling'.

'Mama, what do you mean? Nan was abandoned as a baby?'

By then, her mama was fading. She needed help to wet her lips. The brightness of her eyes had gone. The doctor reassured her she wasn't in pain, but her mind might be in a cloud. It took her two more days to come back to reality. When prompted again, she spoke: 'On the beach among pieces of glass, driftwood, and shells. My grandparents found her. They waited for months, then two more years, to see if any relatives appeared. The police searched the nearby islands for news about castaways, and nothing came, so the authorities allowed my grandparents to adopt her. They named her Ailsa.'

The story sounded strange and mythical, and it unsettled her. Her mama repeated it several times over her dying days. The day before she died, she mumbled, 'As a teenager, I felt trapped like a seal in a fisherman's net.'

Feeling frightened of a future without her mama and circle of girlfriends, she didn't have the mind to ask about her past. Her mama had been like an oyster which she had tried to open with her nails, getting only scraps. Isla gathered that she'd lived and worked as a teenager in a prestigious hotel, where there was a scandal involving a pregnancy and an important client. Of course, he must have been married; otherwise, why send her far away, across oceans and time zones?

Isla's chest pressed hard, and her eyes stung at the memory. There were so many regrets. The stinging nettles and tall grass pricked her ankles, shin, and calves. The jasmine aroma and gravel crunching under her feet signalled new terrain, a hamlet of houses on a slope with terraced gardens and arrays of flowers. She couldn't understand how she got the sign to the summit so wrong.

The place was hidden from the main road because she hadn't seen it when she walked along the beach. Though, six years had passed since the last and only visit to the island. As an angry fifteen-year-old, she'd misbehaved for every minute of the trip to make her mama pay for forcing her to come.

Now, she felt ashamed. She sighed, wishing her mama could have been here doing this walk. She loved painting nature with Isla, their favourite animals, especially deer and red squirrels.

When she reached a tarmacked road, Isla saw a woman coming out of a car and strode towards her. 'Sorry, is this the right way to Goat Fell?'

The woman didn't stop; her overstretched arms carried two bags in each hand. She spoke as she entered her porch. 'Follow the road down until you see the sign.'

Energised, Isla strode off until she found the sign leading her to an open moorland covered in bracken, bramble, gorse, heather, and foxgloves. Further on, mature juniper trees guarded the narrow path snaking upwards, where uneven stones and mud made it difficult to walk in her Converse. The huge boulders to one side, away from the path, were familiar. Yes. She listened; the waterfall and the ravine were nearby. This must have been where she and her mama sat, waiting for the animals to appear, but not even one ventured to meet them.

Voices echoed from the direction of the ravine, and she didn't have to wait long for people to appear. A couple nodded as they passed her by. 'Morning. Good day for walking,' she greeted them, realising it was what her mama would have said.

After they disappeared, she lay across the stone, imagining her mama with proper walking gear beside her.

Her long, curly strawberry hair was in a ponytail, and her blue eyes crinkled in a smile. Isla sobbed hard.

She emptied her rucksack a while later, looking for her water flask. She sipped. She didn't want to wee on the bracken. As a child, a bee stung her bum during a wee on a country walk, and she'd never forgotten about it. A gasp of wind blew away her straw hat, landing in a thorny thicket of bramble and gorse. She couldn't continue without it. She had her mama's genes. Five minutes of this baking sun would be enough to burn her. Nausea rose as she scanned around for a minute or two, but she couldn't see a way to retrieve it.

She groaned. Doubts about not doing the right thing crept up. Two of her mama's friends, whom she saw as aunties, drove her to the airport in silence. When she was queuing at immigration, one said, 'We're here when you return. You're family.' Did they disagree with her trip? And if they did, they were right. Not ready yet.

Isla scoured the path. No one came up or down. She wiped the tears. Her mama would have called it a minor obstacle and would have laughed at it. Intending to get her hat, she stood up. She held the branch closest to it, but a sneaky thorn from a lower limb pricked her legs. Heat spread on her cheeks and body from the effort.

Defeated, she repacked and walked at a pace toward some old trees when she saw him, a red stag, among the tall ferns. She stayed still, staring. His coffee eyes glared back at her. The antler that crowned him forked at the bottom into two, and in turn, each divided into branches that looked like gigantic fingers. She always drew deer with Bambi's eyes, innocent. For a second, he grazed, and she took this as an opportunity to get her camera. The vision would have been majestic if it weren't for the sudden snorting and stomping. Her legs froze, and instinctively, she stumbled backwards. In doing so, she tripped and ended up under the ancient ferns. Her heartbeat galloped. Only birds and insects dared to move. Minutes passed, and there wasn't a sign of the stag, so she sat and crouched, nursing her pride, scratches, and cuts. She assumed the animal had gone, but when she craned her head out of the bracken, she found him watching her direction as if waiting for her to come from her hiding space. He ran toward her, snorting. She dived under the prehistorically large ferns, silent tears pouring down her cheeks. She dared not make a noise in case he was nearby.

One moment, she crouched; next, she sat, hiding her head into her shoulder blades. After going through many emotions, she concluded this was the most ridiculous situation in her life. She was too foreign for this landscape. Anger stirred in her heart against the stag, so she took a stick to defend herself and slowly scrambled to the path leading down to the beach. She ran all the way, glancing back as if chased. In her terror, she hadn't noticed the changes in the sky until the flapping wetness in the air became a downpour, drenching her. Her chest grew lighter. The crested waves transfixed her, reassuring. The sea spray carried her mama's voice and smile when she took her to swim for the first time. Isla recalled the transparent, warm water where little fishes darted between toes and gold sand waited for her in another part of the world. That same water waited for her in another part of the world. Her home was nine hours ahead in time.

MALINA SHAMSUDIN

Striking-up Smoke

When the mayor's wife was found unconscious in her blush Bugatti, the spark of scandal smoked of suspicion. What was she doing alone in the grubby car park of a Save-A-Lot, almost an hour from the Dark Forest?

The local chronicle fanned the embers among residents. Wise to the lines of defamation, the paper reported only the facts: a crushed front fender and a doused passenger seat with remnants of (1) Farmers Market flyers, (2) a scorched cardboard carton once containing 10,000 matchboxes, and (3) a 24" brass candlestick.

Police enquiry is ongoing. The intensive care unit is respecting the privacy of the family.

•

Like most charitable organisations, the Dark Forest Farmers Market was anchored by a bold vision—to empower sustainable, innovative local producers.

Some traders were understandably concerned when the mayor's fiery new wife inherited the reign, but her rule proved far from myopic. This Mrs. Wudkutter had a knack for what sells, and she leaned into the mystical charm the Dark Forest flirted with.

Puppeteering an arsenal of marketing tools, it wasn't long before she had every influencer worth a tote gushing in a reel about the Sunday fete. Like moths to a flame, trendy out-of-towners took to the cobbled streets. Haters hushed as card machines chimed, uniting high street businesses and market traders like the goo of toasted s'mores.

They say Mrs. Wudkutter's acumen came from mastering the psychology of supermarkets. She spotted trends and made bank. Wasn't she the first to graciously grant that witchy baker a stall right after some gingerbread debacle? Now that veganista was blowing up Bakergram and hosting *Flix Bakes with Dame Berry*.

Perhaps this precedent was why traders smirked when Mrs. Wudkutter welcomed an ex-arsonist into the fold. Yati Bakar, trading moniker "Matchstick Miss", was the mastermind behind Strike-A-Match, a startup selling sustainable designer matches that were 100% toxin- and plastic-free. With luxury handcrafted packaging, Strike-A-Match was the perfect pairing for any candle purchase. Matchstick Miss didn't even mind the clickbait: "Reformed pyro still playing with fire". The gawkers always made a token purchase.

While local creatives, food producers and other independent businesses were a draw, influencers kindled a slow burn about "artisan price tags in this economy." Adamant that her market's pricing was always fair, Mrs. Wudkutter nevertheless compromised by encouraging each trader to adopt a "value range" option.

This was easier said than done. For example, while a pop-up candlemaker like Jack B. Nimble could quickly whip up skinnier tealights, Matchstick Miss's already razor-thin margins meant she couldn't compete.

How did Jack put it? "As joyful as safety matches with grumpy goats are at six quid, a penny pincher is going for bog-standard at spare change."

Perhaps that's why Matchstick Miss never said a word when Jack's "hot-seller" gift packs started to feature their own pack of safety matches. They were targeting different crowds.

As the novelty of the notorious Matchstick Miss fizzled out, so did her sales. Concerned traders noticed her dimming demeanour.

"Leap over this candlestick; it'll bring you some luck," the superstitious suggested, but they couldn't spark a smile nor sale. When they became more insistent, Mrs. Wudkutter swooped in to confiscate said candlestick.

The girl seemed to shrink into herself, confidence waning with each customer's cold shoulder. It was almost an act of compassion when Mrs. Wudkutter suggested Strike-A-Match pull the plug for the season. In a public display of solidarity, Jack said he'd had enough of the pop-up and would be leaving, too.

"Bless that spitfire," Jack said. "Some people just aren't cut out for the live markets."

Coincidentally, the day Strike-a-Match said goodbye to the Dark Forest Farmers Market was the last day the mayor's wife was seen in public...

•

Mrs. Wudkutter didn't make it.

CCTV footage showed the mayor's wife pulling into the remote Save-A-Lot, scouring the aisles for a seemingly specific carton of discount matchboxes, and heading back to her car after the purchase.

That's where the most bizarre movements were captured: the Bugatti reversed before shifting gears and ploughing into a parking bollard. CCTV captured a burst of light from the interior of the car, then nothing.

Investigators believe Mrs. Wudkutter must have experienced whiplash from the collision, knocking her unconscious. They also believe the crash must have ignited an unstable budget match, which then self-extinguished within its oxygen-deprived safety packaging. Toxic fume inhalation exasperated in a confined space caused a delayed pulmonary oedema, leading to her devastating demise.

"Thought she was drunk, didn't I," despaired the discount retailer's security, who shared their protocol to leave "this sort of rampant antisocial behaviour" to the authorities.

Police have deemed this a tragic incident rather than arson.

Save-A-Lot has snuffed out its match stock, claiming to have identified the stock's potential to release an abundance of smoke. "As a precaution, and because of our commitment to quality and safety, we are voluntarily recalling the affected matches."

•

Jack pulled away from Save-A-Lot, singed in panic. He could have sworn he'd seen a beetroot Bugatti gunning his way.

No surprise that Mrs. Wudkutter had sussed out that he was bundling mass-produced matches with his candles. Oh, she had asked him about his gift packs at the last market, and he had waxed lyrical about small-town suppliers. Technically, Save-A-Lot was out of town and bulked their wares from global sources—that's how they IKEA'd their savings!

It must have been that sooty Strike-A-Snitch. The Dark Forest Farmers Market was too frou-frou for his oat candles, anyway. Jack was an independent crafter, for crying out loud, not some counterfeit criminal. He had the receipts to prove it.

He crouched low in his seat as he drove past flashing blue lights. Thank goodness he was heading out of this flaming town.

•

Where there's smoke, people will try their darndest to pin the fire. While the police and papers cleared the former arsonist, curls of doubt choked through the mourning Dark Forest Farmers Market. Opting for distance from the drama, Matchstick Miss took the advice of her former trading mates to swap markets for e-commerce.

As a flicker of luck would have it, her practical-yet-stylish matches stole the show in a pivotal fireplace crime scene within a *Flix Murder Mystery*. Glam Mag's review claimed, "When the killer bestie lit that fire with one strike, I knew I needed my own kitschy matches to luxuriate my life."

Strike-A-Match's safety matches with grumpy goats sold out within 24 hours. Bored bears and perky pigs were the next to go. No budget options nor price quibbling were involved. Diversification with painted glass vessels is on the drawing board.

According to Matchstick Miss's small business accountant, her blazing trajectory is set to ignite global demand.

MIRIAM HUXLEY

Manifesting

Ali was about to take the first sip of her first pint of the weekend when the notification popped up on her screen. Her heartbeat snagged a little. *Subject: Re: Application for Job Post 1187F.* She looked around the pub. She was almost alone, besides the old guy who sat in the corner opposite the bar every evening, and a couple of German tourists in hiking gear debating which whisky to try first. Her friends had all messaged to say they were running late, because they, unlike her, actually had jobs and responsibilities. Haha. The jokes were starting to feel less like jokes and more like the lead-up to an intervention.

She looked at her screen again. The notification was still there. Five o'clock on a Friday. If she opened the email now and it was bad news, she'd spend the time until her friends arrived growing more depressed (and drunk), and that would just bring everyone down. Then they'd start talking about how they were worried about her spending too much time alone.

But if it was good news, she could make an announcement, and everyone would cheer and offer to buy her drinks and she'd get happy drunk and probably go home with Simone (even if they both knew it wasn't a good idea). And her friends would go back to genuinely enjoying her conversation rather than just tolerating her endless diatribes about how unfair the job market was and how capitalism was the greatest scam in human history.

She reached for her phone, hand hovering over it.

The interview had gone well. She'd worn her power outfit – a blazer with corduroy arm patches she'd thrifted as a teenager, tartan slacks her mother called 'smart', and a white shirt her friends called her 'pirate shirt' – and she'd shaken hands with all the right people. Her hands hadn't even been that sweaty. Like ten percent clammy. She'd answered all the questions and everyone in the interview room told her how excited they were to meet her – at the beginning and at the end. She'd even seen a sparkle in the line manager's eyes when he said they'd be in touch soon. She'd gone away feeling better about it than any other interview she'd ever had in her life.

Yes. Her whole life.

She took a sip of beer and picked up her phone. She had mostly positive feelings about the situation, but hadn't they mentioned getting back to her at the beginning of the week? She'd been obsessively refreshing her email for days now. And when she thought back to it, hadn't there been a moment where they'd asked her about her greatest weakness – a question she'd prepared and memorised multiple answers to – and she'd laughed and said, 'Weaknesses? Don't know them!' Everyone had laughed at the time, but looking back now, that probably wasn't the best approach to the question, even if she did eventually say something about being a perfectionist who didn't always know when to delegate, blah blah corporate speak. She'd spent the last few days trying to distract herself with reading books she usually never had time for, walks that almost always ended with popping to a little shop or cafe for a treat. She'd tried to stay positive. Weren't her friends always trying to tell her that manifesting was the new hustling?

Just then, the bell on the door tinkled and Simone walked in.

Simone walking into the bar was always an event in Ali's mind, but today it felt like time stopped for a moment, or at least slowed down so Ali saw all the nuances of a smile spreading across the other woman's face. A smile that was just for her. The slightly crooked teeth revealed, the red lips turning upwards, the blue eyes crinkling. And then Simone was at the table and time reverted to its regular speed.

She draped her massive all-weather puffy coat over the stool and sat down next to Ali. 'Oof, I'm late. I was just getting so much done and I lost track of time.'

'No worries,' Ali said, not really hearing Simone as she attempted to look casual from behind her pint glass. Did Simone always look this good? There was something different about her. Ali put the glass back down when she realised her hands were shaking. Simone always had an effect on her, but this was silly. Her heart was clunking in her chest and her cheeks were burning. It wasn't that often that they were the first to arrive. Normally it was all stolen glances across a table surrounded by friends. Eventually, she managed a 'You good?' from behind her glass.

'All the better for seeing you,' Simone answered, winking.

Ali choked on a mouthful of beer.

'I'm going to the bar. You want anything?'

Ali pointed to her half-full glass and shook her head. She watched Simone at the bar. Was she wearing something new? Had she changed her hair? Ali looked away, trying to calm herself by thinking about the email. Rejection was like a cold shower. And it was going to be a rejection. Of course it was. Who was she kidding? Her stupid joke was echoing over and over in her head.

She looked over at the bar, and it seemed as though Simone was walking toward her in slow motion. And that smile … that was a different smile.

'Did you do something to your hair?' Ali asked.

Simone shook her head, and her smile widened. 'Nope.'

'New jumper?'

Simone shook her head again. But the blue of her jumper did make her eyes look bluer, like ridiculously blue. Ali was having a hard time looking away.

When the moment felt like it had gone on for much longer than was comfortable, Ali reached for her phone. The notification was still sitting there. Taunting her.

'You keep looking at your phone. What's up?' Simone asked.

'I've got an email about a job application,' Ali explained, and she kept her eyes on her glass, unable to continue the eye contact that was making her heart feel like it was going to jump straight out of her chest. 'I'm worried it's going to be like all the others. Rejection,' she said slowly, pulling the word apart.

Simone flipped her hair over her shoulder, took a drink, and licked her lips. Then she leaned in, close enough that Ali could feel the soft blue wool against her arm. Simone crooked a finger and Ali leaned in even closer. 'What if I told you there was a way for you to get exactly what you want?' Her breath was hot against Ali's ear.

After a while, she placed a hand on Ali's thigh.

It took Ali longer than it should have to process what Simone had said. She pulled away, frowning. 'What do you mean? Do you know of something I should apply to?'

She'd been forwarded so many potential jobs from her friends, even had a couple of interviews arranged through friends' connections. But the rejection was always the same.

Simone shook her head, and as her blonde hair swayed, Ali was sure she could see little sparks like static electricity flickering around her head.

'No, I mean what if I can guarantee that you get this job?'

Ali's heart thunked faster. 'Do you know somebody? Have you heard something?' It would be just like Simone to withhold a useful contact until the last minute and then casually drop in the potential for nepotism. *Oh yes, my brother's best friend works there. I'm sure he would've given you the job if I'd asked.* So helpful.

Simone shook her head again. More sparks. Then she smiled, and this time, Ali was sure the smile looked different.

'Then how?'

'I can make it happen. If you're willing to listen to what I have to say.' Simone picked up her glass – a tumbler of something dark and viscous, not anything like the pink concoctions she usually ordered – and looked at Ali conspiratorially. 'And you promise not to tell anyone else.'

Ali looked around the bar. The German tourists still hadn't decided, and the old man in the corner seemed to be sleeping, surrounded by empties. None of her friends had arrived. Who was she going to tell?

Simone took another drink and licked her lips, revealing, just for a moment, teeth that looked a lot sharper than Ali remembered. Then she put the glass down and looked serious. 'You can have the job, you can get all your friends off your back and put an end to that secret group chat you've been worried about, and you can go back to being the fully employed, responsible adult we all know you so desperately want to be. But there will be a cost.'

Ali wanted to follow up on the secret group chat – how did Simone know she was worried about that? – but first asked, 'What kind of cost? They told me I could be based in the city – they're not going make me go somewhere else, are they? I don't want to commute again.' Her palms were sweating. She'd do anything to avoid needing to pack her life up.

Simone shook her head. Zap zap zap. 'Not that kind of cost.' She laughed a laugh that was much more femme fatale and much less Office Manager. 'You want the job, don't you?'

Ali looked across the table again, watching little bolts of electricity dance around Simone's blonde head. 'I really do. What do I have to do?'

'That's the best part,' Simone said, and then motioned for Ali to come in close. 'All you need to do,' she whispered, 'is have a drink with me.'

The words sent a chill through Ali. How much had she had to drink?

'And then you open that email.'

'That's it?' Ali pulled away, trying to examine Simone objectively. Had Simone already read the email? Was this all some game? 'Are we manifesting?'

'Something like that,' Simone said, laughing. She raised her glass. 'Chin chin.' Then she clinked the tumbler against Ali's pint glass with just enough force to send a drop of the dark liquid flying into Ali's beer. 'Drink up, darling.'

Ali tipped her glass back, feeling Simone's eyes on her the whole time, and the return of the hand on her thigh.

Re: Application for Job Post 1187F. Ali tapped on the email, her finger shaking. What if it had all been a game and Simone was lying? How could she know what the email said? Despite what her friends said, she didn't think manifesting was really a thing.

'Read it to me,' Simone said, leaning in close.

'Dear Ali, it was lovely to meet you and we're very happy to offer you the position...' Ali let out a strangled kind of laugh.

'Didn't I tell you?' Simone said, and she squeezed Ali's thigh. 'You made this happen.'

Sure, Ali knew she'd been working towards this, that she was the one at the interview, but it felt like this was all Simone. 'No, you made this happen!'

Simone just winked. 'Now, tell me why you're so excited about this job.'

When Ali ran out of things to say and her drink was empty, she offered to buy another round. When she got to the bar, she turned around to see Simone watching her, sparks still flying. Did it matter that her other friends had bailed, saying they were all too busy or too exhausted to make it? She had Simone. She had a job. She ordered another pint but hesitated when ordering for Simone. What had she been drinking?

'One second,' Ali said to the bartender and then bounded back over to the table like the confident, productive, employed human she now was. 'What are you drinking?' she asked Simone.

But Simone was looking at her phone, her brow furrowed. When she looked up, her eyes looked dull, and the sparks had disappeared from her hair. 'What?'

Ali pointed to Simone's empty glass. 'What do you want?' She'd probably just gotten distracted reading a work email.

Simone sighed. 'Oh no, I can't have another. I didn't realise how late it was. I've got to be up early tomorrow.'

All Ali could do was watch as Simone shrugged back into her giant coat, marshmallow once more. The bell above the door tinkled and then she was gone. There was no goodbye kiss, no mention of the next time they would see each other. Simone didn't even congratulate Ali.

But that was fine!

Ali returned to the bar, maybe with slightly less enthusiasm than she'd had only moments earlier. It was totally fine! She could have one drink by herself without worrying anyone. One celebratory pint. She had a job, that was what mattered.

When she sat back down, she looked around for someone to tell the good news.

And then she clinked her glass against the empties on the table.

EMERSON ROSE CRAIG

Give Me My Greatest Desire

Everybody else was driving south. Mile after mile of vehicles crawling, bumper to bumper, with many pulled over to the side. Maya flew down the freeway, the empty lane before her stretching into the horizon. Her chest tightened as she glanced at the small box resting in her lap. She had done her best to avoid this, but now she was the last one left. Every few miles large billboards shot up into the sky, each giving variations of the same message: *Humanity will fall if The Gnik is not satisfied—Bring their greatest desire or all humanity shall suffer the consequences—Failure means destruction.* Thousands of eyes watched her zipping past; their last hope. After all, if one did not watch the world fall, one would be doomed to be unsure of whether or not it had ever happened.

The palace was rather less guarded than Maya expected. Although, upon further reflection, considering that every person left on Htrae had failed in the mission set by The Gnik, most were too nervous to hang around. Maya walked through the empty halls. The floor was lined with large stickers of arrows leading through the maze of hallways. On either side of the path were heaps of objects, cast off after they were deemed failures by The Gnik. Almost anything you could imagine was piled nearly to the ceiling: bright colored sports cars crushed under TVs and leather furniture, brass instruments clogged with jewels and watches, golf clubs draped in sparkling dresses. The overpowering smell of spoiled food stung her eyes; Maya held her breath and carefully traversed the floor littered with torn book pages and broken china. The arrows ended abruptly, leaving Maya in front of a large set of double doors.

Hanging from one of the doors was a sign written in large letters: *Knock with feet and scream, 'I am a pink elephant' for entrance*. Maya did as she was bid. The large door fell forward into a dome-shaped room built of golden bricks. A path stretched down the center of the room, lined on either side with rows of elegant white swans, heads turning in unison to watch her. The swans, it was said, had been brought in after someone tried to gift The Gnik with death. Sitting at the far side was The Gnik, looking small in an oversized throne. The Gnik's skin was stretched too tightly across their face, and their crown towered up, nearly doubling The Gnik's height. As Maya approached, two guards appeared from behind the throne.

"Jump twice." The guards were dressed in identical gold that matched the throne and they kept their faces covered behind bulbous helmets.

Maya complied, the box still clasped firmly in her hands.

"Place your hands on your head."

Again, she followed the instructions, the bottom of the box pressing her hair flat as she held it tightly between her hands.

"Stick your tongue out and blink twice."

When she was done, the guards stepped back, if only slightly.

"Present The Gnik's greatest desire."

With shaking hands, Maya opened the box, raising it for The Gnik to see inside.

Ever so slightly, The Gnik's head dipped to see what Maya had brought. Inside the box was a single piece of paper. Written across its surface in delicate cursive handwriting were the words *Your Greatest Desire*. The Gnik looked at it for a moment before gazing lazily back at Maya.

"This is not my greatest desire. Away with her."

"Wait!" she pleaded. If she failed, they were all doomed. "But I gave you exactly what you asked for!"

"You cheated," came the dismissive reply.

"Then at least tell me what you want! If we have all failed, then it is over anyway!" Maya begged.

"I want my greatest desire." The Gnik leaned over to one of the guards. "Not a very bright girl, is she?"

Maya stared at The Gnik in horror. "You don't even know what it is, do you?"

"Take the failure away," The Gnik said again, clearly bored.

Two of the guards stepped forward, but Maya moved away from them. With a flick of The Gnik's wrist, the swans began to move toward her. She recoiled from their beaks.

"But there is still one person left who has not made you an offer!" she cried.

The Gnik looked at her with a curious expression, waving for the swans to halt.

"You have not made an offer to The Gnik." Maya pointed directly at The Gnik.

The Gnik followed her finger, turning to look before realizing who she meant.

"You cannot enact your anger upon us until every

person has tried to present you with your greatest desire. That is what you decreed."

The Gnik glared at her. "If I wish to make myself a person then I will present myself with my greatest desire. If I do not wish it, then I shan't. Take her away."

The swans moved closer to her, beaks edging toward her tender skin.

Maya choked back a sob. It couldn't just be over. It wasn't fair. The Gnik's request was impossible. Had it all been a game? Did they find it fun to toy with the world before they destroyed it? Maya wanted to scream at them. What did it matter now, anyway? But the swans had already forced her through the palace doors and slammed them in her face.

•

Maya sat at home, dinner simmering on the stove as she worked on her computer, almost two months after facing The Gnik. After the swans had forced her out of the palace she had collapsed next to her car and waited for the end of the world. The following hours had dragged on painfully slowly until the broadcast blasted over the radios. Everyone was to report to the palace to receive a smack on the head with a red yoyo by The Gnik. Alone on the pavement, Maya had only been able to laugh while listening to the broadcast: The Gnik had at last found their own greatest desire. The welts faded within a few days. Many tried to claim that this would have been their second guess for what The Gnik's greatest desire was, but they were ignored.

Rubbing her head absently, Maya tried to focus on the overdue data analysis worksheet on her computer but found herself clicking through links from her social media accounts instead. The article currently on her computer screen was a statement made by the swans the day before, finally addressing the disappearance of The Gnik after weeks of silence. After tying their necks together, they informed the people as one that they had no idea where The Gnik was. But everyone knew swans were liars. They should have said that they knew exactly where The Gnik was, and that would have put the whole thing to rest. Maya could not help but wonder if anyone would remember The Gnik. But that, she supposed, would depend on the outcome of the war between the humpback whales and sugar ants that had taken over most of her newsfeed.

WESTER WAGENAAR

We Do Not Want Him

We do not accept Horace. Of course we don't.

Every year we paint our picket fences to ensure an impeccable white. Every weekend we toil in the soil to create weedless yards bursting with flowers of each hue of the rainbow. Every day people enjoy the view from one of our benches and hear the harmonies sung by birds who pick *our* trimmed trees for their nests.

Can you believe it? Our beautiful neighbourhood. Invaded. By one of them.

We stay put at first, priding ourselves on our patience. Perhaps it is a fluke. Perhaps this guy is merely squatting in the vacant house. We point fingers, perhaps whisper a little behind our hands and peek through our blinds. Isn't that a purely human response when one's way of life is under siege? Then we see the *SOLD* sign and know he is here to stay.

We call an emergency neighbourhood meeting. At the community centre, we rile ourselves up going through every scenario, imagining the profanities he will hurl at us in some incomprehensible accent. Unable to contain our anger any longer, we march straight to his door and mash the doorbell. When he opens the door, clad in a frustratingly average plaid shirt, smiling sanctimoniously, we tell him our thoughts exactly the way we prepared them.

"Let's cut to the chase. Your presence devalues the neighbourhood, so your move is literally costing us money. You owe us."

His smile unwavering, he walks into the house and returns with a box of cookies, which he hands to us. He nods – disturbingly mannered – and closes the door, leaving us simmering.

How dare he try to bribe us! Let alone with cookies. Who knows what he put in them? More importantly, how dare he not acknowledge our concerns? Didn't even deem us worthy of words. Upsetting. No, offensive. That's what it was. A hate crime. Perhaps he doesn't speak our language. That would be a whole other can of worms. All these people coming here and not even bothering to learn the local tongue. Outrageous!

We bide our time. We check his number plate, but his car is legal and passed its periodic inspection just a little over a month ago. Next, we go through his mail, then his trash, searching for unpaid bills and other incriminating evidence. We don't find any.

Our opportunity arrives months later when Horace begins planting conifers around his back garden. We check satellite images and notice he has put them six centimetres over his territory. Obviously, we sue his ass.

In the courtroom we hear him talk for the first time.

"I stand here defending myself," he says, before making his case. "Because of the wide, unmarked path beside my back garden, I misunderstood the borders of the plot of land I bought."

"Bullshit!" we shout.

"Order!" the judge retorts.

Horace continues, "I believe the conifers aren't in the way, as the adjacent path is wide enough to accommodate two passing cars. When I purchased the house, the back garden was a bare grass patch. The conifers add merit to the area."

We bite our tongues, swallowing his insult at our neighbourhood. Besides, we notice how he is charming the judge with his sneaky ways. He has an accent, sure, but his grammar is impeccable, and he uses all the right words to placate her.

"Rules are rules," the judge grumbles, rightfully so, and she orders him to uproot every one of the sixteen conifers and move them back.

We are exuberant, jumping up and down, but he doesn't seem fazed. His calm, accepting smile worries us.

Two weeks later, he hangs a sign above his doorpost: *Cookies & Compliments*. Rows of eerily familiar cookies are put on display on his windowsill. We check the paperwork immediately, but he managed to correctly register his business.

The audacity! First, he gave us those cookies in a mockery of kindness. Now, we are expected to spend our hard-earned money on his business. Of course, we flushed his earlier bribes down the toilet, so we have no clue what his attempts at baking taste like. We don't intend to find out and ensure none of us will. We are good people; our neighbourhood maintains a zero-tolerance policy on betrayal.

For weeks, we patrol the streets to nip his ambitions in the bud and pride ourselves on seeing his cookies go stale. He bakes them again and again, but every batch awaits the same fate. We don't break rank.

The postman cycles into the neighbourhood. An altogether affable fellow, really. One of us. Well, not exactly from our neighbourhood, but he has delivered our mail for years. We share inside jokes, like poking fun of those posh posers one neighbourhood over, exaggerating their rolling r's in jest.

"Thank you, kind sirrrrr," we'd say.

"You'rrrrre welcome," he'd go, a complicit smile on his lips.

But when he delivers mail to Horace, through our binoculars we notice him leave with a mouthful of cookie.

"Let's stop beating ourselves up over this," we decide during the next neighbourhood meeting. "A single customer won't make Horace's shop last."

This is true. Logic dictates it is a matter of time before he will be forced to dissolve the company.

Yet the postman keeps visiting, leaving Horace's house with more boxes than he drops off. He barely even leaves the porch and his fat fingers are already smashing a cookie into his face. These days, his fluorescent jacket has turned chock full of crumbs, a testament to his crimes. His beaming smile is wider than the ones he gives us.

It takes mere weeks for word of mouth to spread like a plague and for people of all ages, sizes, and colours to barge into our neighbourhood. Our homes seem invisible. They don't even look at our freshly painted houses nor notice the newly planted daffodils beside the pond. Instead, they merely scan the neighbourhood, their eyes lighting up only once they spot Cookies & Compliments and the queue snaking out of it.

We know his secret ingredient isn't love, so what is he hiding? What does he put in those cookies to have deceived people this quickly? We need to find out. With heavy hearts, we chip in and visit him to purchase his entire cookie selection.

When it is finally our turn, we confidently squeeze into and fill the house. We expected boxes left unpacked, family portraits of equally foreign-looking folk, and second-hand, tasteless furniture, but his shop is akin to a living room, much like ours. Cosy and homely, we hate to admit. With cinnamon and roasted coffee lingering in the air, it smells the part too. We kick back the knotted rug, yet find no dust underneath.

When Horace looks up at us from the cash register in the corner, his eyes crinkle in recognition. His smile never wavers.

"One of each," we demand.

"Of course," he says, taking the cookies with tongs from plastic tubs and placing each one into a napkin. Next, he singles us out.

He presents John, our oldest, a coconut blondie, telling him, "You have a keen eye for the community."

To Mignon, he gives chocolate chip, and says, "You put a lot of care in your clothing style and it shows."

Ismael, he hands the gingerbread cookie. "I admire your petunias. They're glowing as much as you."

Tamika? Oatmeal raisin. "You're a great mother to your kids, who clearly love you."

We can regurgitate it all, but some were actually swayed by this marketing stunt. During another emergency neighbourhood meeting, they say when Horace handed them their cookie and compliment, they felt seen. That Horace isn't a bad guy. That Horace hadn't judged them, despite everything.

"Besides," they say, "the cookies are out-of-this-world delicious."

Even though we concede the cookies are "not the worst," those dissenters are no longer welcome.

•

The next day, Horace's house is graffitied. *GO HOME*, it reads, red letters running like blood. We all peer out of our windows, watching while Horace climbs a ladder set against the wall, carrying a bucket of paint. Below *GO HOME*, he adds, *I already am, thank you very much*. He even draws a little heart at the end. To our dismay, customers begin posing with the wall for selfies, making peace signs and grinning like braindeads.

The neighbourhood morphs further in a difficult-to-fathom direction. Benches are put outside of Horace's house and shop, occupied by customers spilling out. Those we kicked out of our meetings are among them, chatting with the other guests. Even with windows closed, we hear their hideous laughter.

When John's time has finally come – rest in peace, old man – and his house is put up for sale, it is bought instantly. We want to invite the new residents to the neighbourhood meeting to ensure they do not get snatched by the wrong camp but are appalled to discover they are already loyal patrons of Cookies & Compliments. In fact, the wretched shop was the main reason they moved in.

We begin to stack the unused chairs in the community centre and hide them behind the curtains to keep our meetings from feeling too depressing. However, nuance has been worming its way in.

"I don't like it either, but at least the triple choco one is nice."

"Yeah, it's not all bad. They look at our gardens sometimes."

"I even saw a few stroll through the neighbourhood yesterday."

The rot has crept deep, we realise, making us desperate. The last of us begin handing out flyers. *This is how they get you! The dangers of fake kindness.* We push them onto every customer. Every evening we have to pick them up from the asphalt. A former member of ours even spits at our feet, crumples a flyer, and lobs it at us.

"You lot can't recognise kindness when it stares you in the face."

It takes one final blow for us to fall apart. Our doorbells are rung. Slipper and pyjama-clad, we gather at the community centre, lugging along the red-ribboned boxes we found on our front doormats.

Malee unwraps a bottle of her brandy of choice, and two plushie platypuses, her children's favourite animals.

Jun and Ken play with the leaves of some blue-petaled plant, another addition to their botanical menagerie.

"How thoughtful," Timothy mutters, just above his breath, holding a bunch of foreign stamps his collection must have been missing.

Every box has one thing in common: they all contain a cookie and a written compliment.

"Hey," I say, because I see them cautiously exchanging grins. "Stop and think for a minute. We spent years here, anchored to this place, to each other. And now this outsider is tearing us apart. You know everything about me, and I about you. How did he –"

"What's in *your* box?" they interrupt.

A line has been drawn. I feel sick. Their smiles, once a beacon of hospitality and community, seem distant. I stand up, veer to the trash can, open it, and chuck in my box.

•

Twilight envelops the neighbourhood. As I trudge past the houses, I can hear their blinds smack against windowsills. My attempts to greet familiar faces are met with averted eyes and wide berths. Even the dogs bark their disapproval. When I reach the boisterous hustle of Cookies & Compliments, laughter turns to whispers. Just then, from behind the window, Horace notices me. He smiles, waves, then gives me the thumbs up. I run off, tears in my eyes.

At the next scheduled neighbourhood meeting, I find myself sipping lemonade from a plastic cup, staring at four empty chairs. After an hour, I return home. In my mailbox I find a used Cookies & Compliments napkin, words scribbled on it.

We humbly request you quit visiting the community centre. We will make use of it instead. Kind regards, the Neighbourhood.

THOMAS CARROLL

●

A small, black spot chased the football players around on the TV. It was the FA Cup Final, so that was supposed to be something worth watching. His pals still thought so, the group of them pushing thirty in their own ways; thinning hair, you know. The old five-a-side team not quite in their glory days.

Graeme blinked. The spot stayed. He rubbed his eye and sighed and stood up for another go at the fridge. The last can, and the rest of them were on three each already, so it was only fair. Graeme kept count like that. An empty tub of butter. He smelt the pack of salami and decided against a sandwich.

Loud whooping and groans from the other room. There must have been a goal. Graeme always had a knack for missing all the goals. Back to it then and trying to make the right sort of talk: rubbish pass, what a tackle, that should have been a foul! Graeme used to like watching the football. The pub nights with too many pints and the loud noise of the crowd. Snatches of faces smiling. Years ago. Maya. All of that.

The game finished up and his mates filtered out. They had come to Graeme's because he had the big TV in the big living room. Good job and going well. His friends made little jokes about it: 'Can you get me one, pal?' Laughter.

Everyone liked a bit of banter. He gathered up the empty cans into piles and left them for later. Cracking a window open; the late spring air.

The spot was still there as he brushed his teeth, pockmarking the mirror. Maybe it was from one of those new downlights he had put in in the kitchen. Modern. Way bright. All the better for selling the place, apparently. His mum had been so pleased with the new kitchen, hands clasped and eyes shining at it. Her boy going places. Moving on.

In the morning the spot wasn't gone. And the next day. His eye got sore from rubbing. Those eye drops didn't help. The internet said a lot. A week and it wasn't gone.

In the optician's they had a big thing they looked down, almost like one of those tripods the builders used for the kitchen. The lens stared down his eye. A dumpy level, that was the name. The optician was saying something.

"What was that, sorry?" Graeme said.

A smile twitched at the corner of their lips. "I think we will need to run some more tests," they said.

"Oh, okay, when?"

"As soon as possible, really; tomorrow afternoon?"

The tomorrow afternoon of the end of your life. Graeme sat at home, staring at the wall. There was the spot, just perched happily; maybe it was bigger already. Was two weeks enough for that? They hadn't been able to say, really. Progressive. Degenerative. Fuck.

Nobody knew yet. He gave the same smiles at work. He had the same nonsense conversations with his friends. After another week, he found himself telling his mum; just spurting it all out when he went to visit. She cried for hours, sat in the little cottage, the sunken sofa, a cup of tea getting cold. Graeme hugged her like he hadn't for twenty years. Unashamed, tight and hoping.

The horrible hoping, like maybe it wasn't getting that bad; only one spot and he could still see the rest of things, yeah. Doctors can be wrong. But the months changed that; the growing spot changed that. Wanting to scratch at it, wanting to pick it out. The fuzzy edge closing in and flashes of light when he was trying to sleep.

There were support groups. A leaflet. Eventually he would have to talk about it. He went to one and heard the stories and they had so much to say. Graeme didn't have stories like that. As though his life wasn't good enough to be ruined in the first place.

When he did start telling other people, those various people in his life, they looked at him in a sort of way. A creased brow, downward mouth sort of way, like they really felt how sad it was. How sad; how holy shit I'm glad it isn't me. And suddenly, there was only one person he really wanted to tell, staring at the number on his phone – if it was even the same anymore, if she would even pick up – but he couldn't bring himself to press dial.

Trying to cry. Apparently that was good. The office with the sofa and the calm art and the calm walls that he wanted to tear a hole through. And how was he doing? And how did he feel? And how was that going? And how did he feel?

I don't know. I don't know this world anymore. People anymore. I don't know myself anymore.

Desperate lonely moments at night. I just want my eyes back. Squeezing the pillow. I just want my eyes. I just want hands to hold me. I just want her hands. I just want her.

Work let him go; some money. A lawyer in a room that he had not seen before. Please sign here. They had a volunteer with a big smile and a lanyard making sure that the blind person understood what was going on. Graeme wanted to shout at them but couldn't bring himself to bother.

Drifting. Another doctor's appointment. Yep, bad news.

He got used to people holding his arm. He got used to the slow way they would speak to him. The light was the spot now, and blurry. Funny crayon shapes of people, his flat, the things he used to know. It was hard to remember any of it anymore. Maybe his ears were better: Batman. Maybe his nose was better: Stinkman. Maybe food tasted even worse.

His mum took him to get some shoes like he was a child again, and the person asked her, 'What colour does he like?', as if he wasn't in the room. I like bright fucking pink. Unicorns. Give me the sparkly ones that play a song when you jump. Stuttering reply. His mum telling him to stop. You got any of those then? Size ten? He made the girl cry. Silence in the car back and he just wanted to explain, and how?

They were trying to get him a dog. He didn't know if he wanted a dog. Maya had wanted a dog. Another disagreement. Little bricks pulled out of the bridge until the whole thing fell down. He could see her on the other bank, her face suddenly close, suddenly far away. If only he could shout loud enough, he could tell her, and she would know, and maybe it would be okay. Maybe she could fix it because nobody else could, and all he wanted was for somebody to fix it and to take it away.

Please put me back together again.

Long dreams. He slept because what else. The TV was an insane friend in the corner. Locked up too and babbling.

And on. And trying to make the best of it. And maybe

giving up. And he still hadn't brought himself to call. And maybe getting used to it. Slowly. Like you could get used to everything with enough time and no way of doing anything about it. Or not used to it but at least not angry. Or still angry but not making it everyone else's problem anymore. There were worse things, sure.

And then a year. So quick. It had gone how they said it would, the world now a vague smudge. Oh well. Today he had his mates around him. Another FA Cup Final. That was good. His mum here too, responsible for it all, setting him down a beer. He wasn't supposed to drink. Thank you, Mum. A little squeeze of his shoulder. His friends were making a show of talking about the football. Banter like nothing else was going on.

The doorbell rang. He hadn't thought there was anybody left.

"Who is it, Mum?" he called out, worrying. A random stranger. No eyes to know.

His mum didn't reply. Two pairs of feet. There was a smell he recognised, a smell that went right to his brain, right through him. He remembered the bottle. He remembered getting it for her as a present. And then his heart was going, quick in his chest.

"Who is it?" he asked again, voice quiet. The whole room quiet. He knew.

She crouched before him. A hand. He gripped it tightly, the first solid thing in forever, and the tears came like they hadn't before.

"I'm sorry," Maya said. "I'm so sorry."

TESS SIMPSON

The Winter Class

We sit in five rows, each with our own individual desks. The desks are wooden, and the chairs are wooden, and the floor is made of long wooden boards, so when we enter the room there is a symphony of creaking. We enter in our rows, four at a time, and once we all sit, there is silence.

We sit for the entire day like that, and the only indication of the time passing is the stretch of the shadows across the room. We cannot have a clock, because a clock ticks.

There is a board at the front of the room, and when we enter each morning, a question is written on it. We must spend the rest of the day answering it. Sometimes the question will only appear once, and the next day it is replaced by a new question. Other times the question sits on the board for days. Sometimes for weeks.

There is no order to the questions that appear on the board. There have been straightforward ones, for example:

'What is the length of a year?'

This appeared on a day when the sun shone a watery yellow light through a grey blanket of clouds.

Or:

'Where does the wax in a burned candle go?'

On a day the sky was so deep and blue it hurt to look at.

Or:

'What are the consequences of winter?'

On a day the windows were obscured by fog.
They are sometimes hard:
'**What is the purpose of memory?**'
'**What are the methods by which hope can be measured?**'
'**Why are cats so difficult?**'
The questions may not always make sense, but they must always be answered.

The others who sit in the room aren't always the same either. Sometimes someone in the rows has changed. They are no longer tall with thin blonde hair and spots, but instead short, with black braids and dark eyes. We never acknowledge these changes – perhaps it is impolite, or perhaps it is the memory of one of the questions.

The memory is of a dark morning, with grey in the sky and rain splattering against the windows like thrown fruit. We filed in, eyes down, and once the wood had settled back into silence, we looked up at the board.

'**What makes a person unique?**'

The board asked. We read the question and then we began to answer.

The answers are the only thing that changes every day. The removal of the question from the board is contingent on the production of a satisfactory answer. If, the next morning, the question has remained the same, then we know more is required. We must come up with something new.

'**What makes a person unique?**'

remained on the board for fourteen weeks before a satisfactory answer was produced. As is the custom, none of us know who produced the right answer. It could be theorised that the satisfactory answer is derived from the combined results of several of the answers produced by the room. Theorised, that is, if the board asked the question. The board contains the only questions worth asking.

'What makes a person unique?'

is memorable not only for the length of time it took to produce an answer, but also for one of the methods attempted to solve it. In the middle of the work, one of the others stood up – actually *stood* – and spoke aloud.

'For this reason.'

It was all they said.

The next day the other in the second seat, third row back was not the same as they had been the day before. We understood. We continued our work.

We continue our work. We sit in our seats and answer the questions the board asks.

Today we are answering the question:

'Why is there light in the sky?'

A complex question, with many possible answers. We are working when the desk creaks.

This is impossible, of course. The desk has never creaked once we've all assumed our seats. And yet today, something is different.

There is a scratch on the desk, a roughness incongruent with the pattern of the wood. It has not been noticeable before because the chair has never creaked before. There has never before been a need to look down, away from the board.

The roughness is incongruent, but it is orderly. There is a pattern to it, a structure. Here, away from the board, another question is being posed.

We answer the board.

The day shimmers with heat, the air inside the room thick and heavy. Today the board is asking:

'What is the danger of curiosity?'

Perhaps the scratches do not compete with the board's question. Perhaps they form part of the answer.

Tracing them is the solution, it transpires. Their secret is revealed: a series of letters. Language, though it does not match the language of the board. It takes time to decipher, time that should be spent answering the board. The lure of novelty is strong.

It takes the better part of a day to decipher them:

'Argyll. The Summer Class.'

Clarity leads to chaos. An answer is provided that leads only to more questions. Questions and answers.

'What are the characteristics of tartan?'

Asked on a day when the leaves began their shift of pigment from green to red.

'What is the sequence of the seasons?'

Asked on a day when the wind was so strong it blew the branch of a tree into the window and cracked the glass of one of the panes.

'What is a community?'

Asked on a day so cold the frost had coated the inside of the windows.

A flash of understanding. **We are looking for answers, but we are not the first. I am in a cold room and the chair creaks as I shift and I breathe and the air is dry and rough, like it is wrong somehow, like this air does not want to be breathed, to be passed from nose to lung to blood to bone. This air was not made to be breathed by the living. The room is silent, oppressively silent, a silence that no living creature can create or endure. I ache, I ache a bone-deep ache that starts in the soul and radiates outwards, encompassing every part of me. I ache and I move and the ache subsides.**

The table creaks. Rough scratches on the wood. A memory; the scratch of a woollen jumper against my skin. A memory; the softness of a breeze against my face as I turn like a flower towards the sun. A memory; the earth warm and friendly beneath me, the dry soft grass compressed into a bed, and it is so pleasant to be there in the world. The sky above is so blue and so vast it looks like you could dive into it, like it is an endless pool to be savoured.

I remember that there is a world and I remember that I want to be in it and I remember there were terrible times and struggle and pain but I also remember the kind soft grass, and the tingle of salt hitting a cut on my skin as I fish a starfish from a rockpool, and I remember the smoke of the campfire and how it stung my eyes but how it also soaked into the wool of my jumper until it cradled me like safety, and I remember calling a name across the fire and waiting with eagerness for a response, I remember a name and the wool of the jumper and the warmth beneath a vast black sky, and I remember the stars and their brightness and the sun and its warmth, and I remember the fires and the floods and the fear, and I remember the world and its entirety and its end and its loss and the choice that was made the choice that I did not make but I must bear it I must become a thing to bear it and the world we lost it we must find it again we must remember we must answer we must learn and the world and the world and the world I want to stand I want to run I want to scream the chair creaks and the desk creaks and the floor creaks and they all scream in unison as they join my cry as I am standing as I am shouting as I am screaming as I as I as I as I I I I I I I I I I I I I I I

We enter the room every morning with our heads down. We sit in five rows, each with our own individual desks. The room is always the same, but sometimes the others change. There is a desk with a series of scratches on it, third row back, two from the end, and someone sitting there now has hair the colour of the sun.

We look up.

HANNA-MARIA VESTER

A Sleep

Night's teeth were gnashing and I had to get away, out of the house, into the dark. I saw him right when I pulled the door shut and stepped into the street. We walked beside each other.

> I turned to him. 'Are you Canadian?'
>
>> 'You're thinking of a moose. I'm a stag.' His step remained steady.
>
> 'Oh, sorry.'
>
>> 'They're huge.'
>
> 'You're huge.'
>
>> 'I'm average.'

He stopped and his globe-like eyes suddenly seemed sad, gazing at the few windows that were still lit. I didn't know if I could touch him, his soft antlers, his fur. He went on and I followed.

>> Globes illuminated, he sighed. 'I am no safe-house.'
>
> 'No. Who said you should be?'

'Poets. My family.'

Something lingered in the corner of my eye. My university reading slid into view. 'But Elizabeth Bishop was talking about a moose. And you said you're not a moose.' I, however, couldn't help but be a-moose-d. 'Did you run away from home to *become* a moose? To–'

> 'To look at the houses you built, for inspiration you mean?'

He laughed. It sounded like a hoarse cough. I liked it; it made me want to forget tight teeth and join in.

Instead, I said: 'I'm glad to follow you.'

> 'Oh, I thought we were walking beside each other, as equals.'

'Yes. Then I'm glad I went out and happened to find you.'

> 'I was waiting.'

'For me?'

> 'For something.'

'Something. Something would be nice.'

We passed the park that was usually filled with dog walkers, sometimes even at night. That's how you know how godly the hour was. It was the time when absolutely everyone, able to, sleeps.

> The corner of my eye felt itchy again: 'Shouldn't we be sleeping?'

'I hardly ever sleep these days.'

'I think I may be entering those days.'

'Welcome.'

A soft smile, or something like it, descended upon me like a blanket, gently creased by his profundo.

This time, I stopped.

He turned to look at me, antlers swaying.

'How does it end,' I burst out. I couldn't help it.

'How ... How does ...'

'Yes, how?'

I kept staring into his eyes. I had never seen anything so clear, so honest. He kept looking past my left shoulder. I don't know why I asked, because I didn't want an end, I didn't want to know, and I certainly didn't want the truth.

Does it end with a hug? A gasp? With beauty?

Out of the house, into the night, a shot in the dark.

HANNA-MARIA VESTER

Crowded

There once was a lonely maiden, waiting for her prince, or her princess, or, you know, for someone. She lived in a beautiful, overpriced flat in a gentrified area close to the forest. Each day, she would wander among the trees and collect pine cones and acorns to give them a new place to lay their weary heads.

•

One day, upon returning home with her bounty of nuts and seeds, the maiden heard a little voice. She inspected the forest trinkets – had another elf or speaking worm found its way to the human world? But no, here they lay in her hands, still and silent.

The voice returned: 'Hello, over here!'

Words! The maiden could make out actual high-pitched words! She began to look around. Under the cushion? No. In the waste basket? Nothing. The potted plant? Nope. The mirror? It held no secrets.

'I'm over here!'

The maiden spun around. The voice came from her wall. There, in the only framed oil painting she owned (a gift from a long time ago), right next to the projector she used to transplant sitcoms to the wall. There, nestled in the painting, among the coarse oaks, the spindly pines and the glossy moss – a little creature. The branches, high up, allowed for enough damp sunlight to illuminate: a bright orange, tiny human shape with the loveliest hair and the brightest smile. Its little feet stood steadfast on the soft, cross-hatched ground.

The maiden and the creature both bowed, a sign of respect in the forest, nice and slow (like softly pulling a branch or tickling a mushroom, like shaking the hand of a leaf). A mutual, respectful silence took shape between the two.

'I want to make a home!' the creature announced suddenly.

'Of course! In the forest, you mean? I can get you there.' Fingering the pine cones and acorns, the maiden instinctively turned to the window towards the forest up the hill.

The creature knocked on the frame of the oil painting it sat in and let slip a comedically loud cough. 'Oh no! Too far! And I'm already in one!'

The maiden slowly dragged her eyes away from the window and turned back to the painting. She leaned forward and looked past the creature into the carefully constructed coppice.

'Why yes, you are! I suppose it has potential.'

The creature wiggled its little toes, expectantly. The maiden thought for a moment while the wiggling grew ever more frantic. Straightening her back, the maiden said, 'Why don't I make it bigger for you? It must be awfully crowded in there!'

'Why yes, yes!' The creature nodded vigorously, toes wiggling wildly. 'It is, it is so, so crowded!'

•

The maiden-turned-painter walked between the tables and shelves, calmly browsing with an adventurous air. The art supply store was busier than usual: tons of children, eager to papier maché butterflies. Parents, ready to disappear into glitter. Art students, hunting for inspiration. Or just the right yellow.

An air of possibility. And total chaos.

The paintermaiden had left her dwellings (and her new roommate) early this morning. Her coat swung behind her like a tail, twitching ever so slightly. Her frock, a fox's ear in the night, ready to get sprinkled with paint.

She knew what she was looking for. 'These two.'

She stopped next to a table littered with frames and canvases. The salesman gazed at her as if basking in sunlight, name tag glistening on his apron.

He wrapped the chosen, stuccoed frame and bright canvas carefully. 'Enjoy, love.'

The maiden smiled: 'I intend to!', and readied herself to capture the forest yet again. This time, not by gathering seeds, but with her brand-new brushes.

The forest drenched her in an intoxicating quiet.

Work was calm. Crickets sang. The green sat just right.
Work was easy. A blackbird provided helpful pointers.
Work was done.

Re-entering her overpriced abode, a voice greeted her.

'Hello, cheerio, g'day, 'ello, boom boom!'

She smiled at the extravagance. 'Hello, little one. How was your day?'

'I enjoyed walking and whistling and catching worms, thank you very much!' the creature boasted, trying to lift a log in its framed forest-y home. It pulled a face. 'Heavy!'

The maiden laughed. 'Look what I brought you! So you have more space!'

She hung the new picture next to the first. Wood touched wood. The creature stared, mouth agape, eyes glistening.

'Oh, oh, oh! For me!'

The maiden clapped her hands with joy. 'Absolutely! I even painted a little bench for you.'

The creature strode into the second painting. 'Yes, this will do nicely.'

•

The maiden soon went back to the same store. She liked her routines. They comforted her. The same old salesman, the same lovingly organised chaos greeted her. 'Here you go, young lady! Enjoy!' She nodded, strapping the new set of canvas and frame to her handcart: 'I hope so.'

And the maiden headed to the forest to find other parts, bits and bobs, trinkets and trophies that the creature might need.

Work was calm.
Work was easy.
Work was done.

Opening the door to her flatshare, a freshly dried, brand-new painting under her arm, the maiden heard a deep growl that quickly turned high-pitched. 'Is it time to oil the hinges again? ... I'm home!' She entered the dining room and stumbled. Under her feet lay her acorns and pines, sprouting. 'Oh hey.' She kneeled down, brows furrowed. 'I see you are helping me. How lovely of you...' Straightening, she looked to the wall to find the creature. Nowhere to be seen. Off on its own adventures. The maiden hung the picture and proceeded to the kitchen. When she returned with a cup of tea and a microwave-meal, the creature was already snoozing in the new painting, high up, tugged snuggly into one of the branches.

The maiden fired up her projector and watched *Parks and Rec* and *Abbott Elementary* until deep into the night, on mute, so as not to wake her little friend.

•

The old salesman smiled like a question. His nametag had dulled.

'En... enjoy.'

The maiden dragged the easel, the canvas and herself to the forest to paint.

Work was calm
        easy
        etc.

The living room wall was now completely filled with frames. The creature squealed and threw its tiny body from canvas to canvas, luxuriating in its expansive paradise. The maiden sat on the sofa surrounded by old, half-drunk cups of tea. She lifted a fresh one to her lips and smiled weakly.

At night, the grumbling returned, transformed into a roar. She lit up the paintings with the projector, just in case. *Friends* in a *Full House*, laughter bouncing from tree to tree.

In the morning, the maiden's head bore moss imprints from hitting the wall one too many times.

•

The salesman handed her his last remaining frame and canvas for cheap and watched the maiden disappear into the forest.

ALEXIA WDOWSKI

Invitation to the Wedding

So I'd heard that weddings were stressful, and to be clear, I'm not up for any of that. I'm inviting my family from under the sea, and he is inviting his mountain people. They bring the wind and rosemary; my people bring the spines. These are my welcome guests, and there are pleasant times ahead. I am ready. Ready for our life together.

My husband-to-be tempts me out from the seas and dries out my limbs and licks love from my scales. I bring a basket woven from seaweed, sung from everything I've ever known, and he brings his armour, spiky, precious and gold.

Mary tears her way out of my basket, where she is hidden so well, and climbs into his suit with her claws. She whispers to him how she follows me still, and the thought of her fills me with stones hard and blue. Stones fill my throat, fill my eyes, sink me back under the waves. The dark ocean floor welcomes me home, calm with shadow, slow as bones. I search along the smooth grey edges of rocks to find a sharpened corner of a sharpened shell to dig a nest to sleep in. It gets deeper and deeper, and I roll myself inside, and soft sand is my pillow and I nestle in deeper still and cover my eyes and mouth with seaweed. Salt and wet. I cannot move, he cannot find me, and there is no scent to show him the way. Just cold ocean waves lapping forever under a steely sky. 'Pile her ears up with soil,' I hear Mary say from high above the waves, 'Bite her finger roots until they bleed and come apart in her mouth. She will lie alone, forgotten under heavy, dreamless waters.'

The mountains call, though they are not mine yet and I have no claim to them. I can hear the rosemary whispers. I can hear the airwind blow. The scent of pine reaches me like a calling from another world, and I remember the pure violet clouds that rise up before a blanket of snow. I rise with them. To get to my wedding, I surge up from my grave, my hands push through and push out, slick with long wisps of sand that trail behind me, calling. My hands meet the surface and grab.

My nails tear apart in clay-yellow clumps, and I cough up sea worms, one after another, pink and juicy, they fall from me. When they hit the ground, they delicately lift their heads in greeting to each other like they have been lost for a long, long time. My dress is drenched dark with the rich salt of sea, and it clings to my body as I wrestle the rest of me forward. Eventually, I lie, spent and ready, looking up at sharp lights winking through a canopy of trees. I always wanted to be married under the cover of trees. Something that has been here for so much longer than me. Everything that happens to them is in the interior, all movement underground.

The slope feeds itself down into a hollow, and I stumble along pathways, on my way. My people, as they arrive, follow close behind but hidden, fleeting shadows in the bushes. They mark the way, and I know they have been here before me, treading thorns into their own feet to save mine. I feel the soft moss from overgrown headstones and find my path, my feet bound with vines and threaded with wild garlic that tears as I move forward relentlessly. Some statues are broken, others remain intact. Why should they stand? Why should anything old come with us now? I take my weapon, my sharp sea self, where she cannot go, and smash slabs of stone to splinters. She knows I am coming now; I am cold and ready. Long behind me, the pocked stone anchor drags me down. I haul it along and am careless with its mutterings. I bring it too. 'Come with me. If you are here already, you may come.' My anchor cracks open wide.

Out fall flocks of green birds. 'I was expecting you,' they say. 'Why did you take so long?' They say, 'You will be late for your own wedding.' They chatter as they plummet through the trees like hot stones into water, and I follow them through the forest. Mary is in front of me now. She leans on her secateurs, watching the show, chewing her gum at a pace, and our eyes meet. Her eyes are both the blue of a pale winter sky and the green-dark depths of the sea. I can't tell what she's thinking. I can't ever know what she will do. Dizzy and breathless, I offer her up a meaty slab of my heart. It is all I have left to give her.

'Are you ready for your new life?' she says, and I don't know what she means but fear it and have my weapons close at hand to strike her. Always have weapons poised and ready, and know how far down you can breathe.

Before I can smash her, too, into splinters of my past selves, my husband-to-be appears. He stays my arm. 'Let her be.' He pulls my sea mist body towards him. He pretends not to notice the grime and wet and dirt from where I have been, and as he kisses me, our mouths fill with the soil of cedar forests, and we hum a little tune. He pushes my heart back inside me and zips it up carefully. Protected. So we stand together for a while, and I drop my weapons into the mushroom-soft grasses with muffled thuds, and the old woman, who thinks she has power over me, leans over from the shadows and watches us and pulls her chewing gum out into a long, long falling line, winding it around us and pulling us towards her. She keeps pulling us along, and we struggle in the sticky, messy loveliness of how we are joined together, and the graves wait for us, teeming with life, and I say she can come to the wedding because how can she not? We are stuck together, and who can say why we do the things we do?

On the day of the wedding, my cake is red velvet, layered, tiered. You cut it open, and it starts to bleed. My guests sway in time, handing out herbs and seaweed; their dresses are tattered, their feet cold and silent. Beads of liquid glisten on their skin, and they leave moist silver trails on the forest floor. I keep my eyes open wide, scanning for warnings, but the sky is streaked pink and the trees are stable. There are children at the wedding, nieces, nephews, children of friends; they hunt in the woodland and play. They find flowers and interesting pieces of bark and sometimes a feather, and they will bring these to their adult to hold. They run over the graves in little white dresses like little white gasps. They eat all the cake and lick the platter of crumbs and ask for more. There will always be more cake, and crumbs from cake line the winding pathways like confetti. The graves surrounding us sink sideways now; they have settled right down into themselves, comfortably into the ground to wait. I see Mary sitting beside one, too, a feather-green hat on her head, dressed to impress. She is perching, expectant, a green bird on a branch before flight.

She pulls me aside, her eyes burning bright, hot coals. 'When you are dead, I will bury you in my garden, bury you anywhere but here, let the cats prowl over you and all these families forget where you are and who you have been and who will you be and give all the love and the flowers and longing to the living.' I hold my bouquet closer til the thorns tear my flesh. The rain falls and kisses my face and runs in rivulets down my sleeves. The living, breathing part of me feels the slick wet of stems and the already dying skin of the plants in my hand. The rosemary crushes and releases its scent. I remember. I hold time in my hands, clasped. A bouquet of spines, thornily fused, letting each other have their way.

As my husband and I walk together, united, self-conscious, completed, I see Mary one last time, on the back of a motorbike, Mary in the dappled sun, and she's leaving, roaring down the hill. Back to the town, back to the houses. Not yet, I think. I can't follow you today, not yet. In our future, maybe we will burrow underground, making tea and leaving empty cups everywhere, and the soil will drop into every teacup, and we will stir it in together and drink the grit, and it might loosen or stick in our throats, and as old women together we could smile with soily brown teeth and whisper dark, dark secrets. All that is to come.

Today, I'm breaking open, trailing like white streaks of sun, my spine cracking like rocks and becoming something new, and another creature stands here, gold and aflame. This creature couldn't know a thing. This creature was born today, made of both of us. I clawed my way out of my watery grave to breathe and live in the hot, wet sky. The long strands of a weeping willow brush my hair. Silver darts blink goodbye through the leaves. She's leaving us here, today, as we keep writhing forward, encased in each other and the new dewy world, scented, wild with light.

M. H. MONICA

Where the Flowers Fall

The sun plays among the clouds as I do with my big sister, Malli. The Gulmohar tree sways with the wind, its bright red flowers showering all over Malli and falling into the well. Green fields extend to one side, the breeze blowing the leaves of the corn like a ripple through water. On the other side, the barn and house stand as they have for decades, the slate roof providing much needed relief in the summer. Grandpa is nowhere to be seen. He's probably with Ma, asking her how city life has been treating us.

I watch from a distance behind the banyan tree as Malli crouches near the well, hands covering both eyes. She always counts slowly to give me plenty of time to hide, so I decide to take advantage of it and go as far as I can. As I turn around to run, I nearly bump into the tyre. We had hung it from the tree four summers ago. Well, Grandpa did most of the work while Malli and I jumped around in excitement. We played endlessly on it, swinging each other back and forth and round and round till we were sick in the stomach. And each evening, after she and I were so dizzy we couldn't take a step forward, we would collapse in the grass, shaded by the tree, and watch the blues of the sky turn orange and pink. I glance back and notice Malli's dress is also orange and pink. Very pretty.

I slip into the chicken coop and realise what a terrible mistake I have made. She would easily find me here. There would be no space for me to run before she could catch me. As I turn to leave, I notice the few hens in the coop stare at me in bewilderment and begin squawking loudly. I laugh. The chickens, with their comical faces and distinct expressions, have always seemed so unique. I remember when Ma helped Grandpa build this coop six years ago when I myself was six. Grandpa was in awe as Ma made little slides for the eggs to drop to a spot that would be easy for him to pick up. She even brought straw and grass to line the hens' nests so they would be more comfortable. That summer, we had more eggs than we could eat, exchanging dozens of them with our neighbours for rice and different vegetables.

As I move further away from the well and to the barn, I see a sparrow's nest in a hole in the wall next to the barn window. It wasn't there the previous summer. Moving closer, I wonder if there are baby sparrows in the nest. The mama sparrow takes flight at the sight of me. There are two tiny eggs inside. Maybe they'll hatch before summer ends. I go to the barn and expect the smell of dung to hit me, but it doesn't. Maybe expecting it reduces its impact… That's when I notice a new calf.

So much has changed in one year! New chicks, new sparrows, new calves. As I inch closer to the baby calf, he gets skittish and hides behind his mother. His mother, Lakshmi, is also startled but realises it's just me and moos.

I smile. Lakshmi's baby looks exactly like she did when she was a calf. Three years ago, during Pongal, we visited Grandpa's for the harvest festival and the games happening in the village. That's when Lakshmi was born. Smaller than other calves we had seen, she had seemed so fragile. But within a few days, she was running and prancing with such speed that my sister and I could not keep up! Malli and I had fought the entire vacation on who would get to name the baby calf. Ma had convinced my sister to let me name her since I was younger by three years. But I'll tell Malli to name this calf. It's only fair.

I look out the window and notice orange-pink. Rushing outside, I'm shocked to see it's evening already. I wonder how long I've been wandering around the property as I head back to the well. I see my sister walking away. She must have finished counting and searching, too. I guess I won! I call out to her, but she doesn't turn back. She seems to be wiping away something from her face. She has left something by the well. Looks like a note. She walks into the house, ignoring my shouts. Reaching down, I grab the note and read it in annoyance.

•

My Dearest Ro,

This summer hurts more than I thought it would. I miss you still, more than you can ever imagine. I look around the house and see the things we shared, the food we made together, the memories that I shall never take for granted.

I keep thinking the pain will reduce over time, but it comes back in waves, hitting me when I least expect it.

Especially every night when I wait for sleep and instead think of you. Think of summers past and the summers that could have been. Think of how singing *Roja* songs annoy you (even though they are exceptional).

No one understands how much I'm hurting. Ma and Grandpa are hurting in their own way. I see it when they look at our tyre-swing. Lakshmi had her first baby. We would have fought to name him. Now, I must name him by myself. And every new calf that is born. It's not as fun to do so without you here. Nothing is as fun without you here.

I have been blaming myself for what happened that summer three years ago, but I know there's nothing I could have done. I know I must accept it as life, as fate, but I can't. Not yet, at least. I hope you won't forget me even though I know you must. You must find peace and happiness where you are now – among the stars. But I do hope, once in a while, you'll spare me a thought.

I shall long to hear your voice again, to see your kind eyes again, to feel your warm hugs again. And when I'm done mourning your loss, perhaps I shall finally be able to set you free...

Your 'Mal'eficent Malli

•

I look up and see my sister returning with flowers on a plate. She stands next to the well, throwing in one flower at a time. The pink and orange dress flutters with the wind. Her face looks like stone, frozen in time. I see she is older than I remember; her round cheeks are replaced by sharp features. She looks a lot like Ma now.

Looking around the grounds, their familiarity clashes with uncertainty. Peeking inside the well, I don't see my reflection, only flowers of every colour floating around. I vaguely remember that evening. I was wearing my favourite blue and purple skirt. It had suddenly gotten so cold…

Malli is going to miss me, I know. And I'm going to miss her too. The fear of spending eternity around this well by myself grips me. What am I to do? I call out to her desperately. The wind picks up speed, blowing her hair around with fervour. She places the plate at the edge of the well and tries to tuck the flyaways behind her ears. The colourful flowers begin to blow off and fall into the well and on the ground.

Why can't she see me? If she misses me, why can't she sense me standing right next to her? Her tears of sadness mix with frustration as she groans at her hair. I remember that groan. She had made the same sound when I got to name the baby calf. I was wearing my favourite blue and purple skirt. We had yelled and fought that evening by the well, pushing and shoving each other, and she had… And now she says she misses me.

The wind picks up speed. The plate loses balance and falls into the well. She looks in to see it disappear into the darkness and hears the splash. I don't want to do this alone. I don't want to wander around Grandpa's land alone. A strong gust nearly pushes Malli over the edge…

And I call out to my sister. She steadies herself in time, gripping the edge of the well tightly, her face and knuckles turning white. I recognise the fear in her eyes. I had felt it once too...

I tell her not to hurt anymore. I tell her I'm okay and everything will be fine. I tell her to take care of Ma. I tell her I'm okay with her naming every calf from now on. I tell her I'll always be there for her. I'll always love her. I try to reach for her, but my hand passes through the wind.

Our eyes meet. Tears trickle down her face. As the warm breeze blows, the leaves of the corn ripple. And our tyre-swing moves gently with the wind.

ELENA SIMS

Application for Solvers of World Peace

My twin brother is the one with a scrunched-up body. Arthrogryposis – try saying that out loud. Bent hands that can't hold. Skinny legs that can't walk. His wheelchair is electric.

A few months back, his neighbour stopped him outside.
You brought home a baby last week, she said. Is he adopted?
No, my brother answered. He's mine.
The woman gaped while looking over the fresh bundle for further evidence.
When she finally left, my brother's wife asked, What the hell did she think was under my shirt the past nine months?

Laugh about it. That's the better option.
Don't dwell on how out of tune the world is with our melody. Society still treating disability like some Shakespearean tragedy.

But how can you go on living like that?

A friend of mine asked once if I was particular about rubbish.
Why? I asked.
Because you're obsessive, they said.

Oh, that's right. Obsessive-compulsive disorder only means aversions to the vast 'unclean'.
No, I replied. I don't mind touching rubbish. Or public surfaces. I have a problem with buses, but it's not an OCD thing. Humans are nasty. COVID still exists.
My friend insisted, But I've seen you use hand sanitizer. What can I do?
Buy some plastic gloves to better fit the image.

I'm the twin sister with a scrunched-up brain.
OCD – don't you dare attempt to put that in alphabetical order.

By the way, have you heard about how vaccines give babies autism?
Nonsense! – news articles, social media, scientific fact persisted. No one should believe an injection can cause something so horrific.
Wait, back up – the worst situation people can think of is becoming neurodivergent?
Ableism is so layered; people hardly even realise they're doing it.

Let's take Edinburgh for example. Beautiful medieval city. Do you have a ramp? I asked the barista at the fifth café I'd attempted. My brother is coming to visit and not a single place is accessible.
She shook her head.
(This is what happens when cities care more about sandstone survival than fellow flesh and blood. You get shops that haven't compromised since the days witches were being burned in the square.)
Damn, I said then walked out the door. Stopped.

It hadn't felt *right*.
Retreating inside, I repeated the action. It took four times in total. Irrational, obviously. The way I exit a shop won't actually protect me from a bus filled with filthy, germy people if it decided to swerve. Still, OCD often speaks louder than logic.
The barista paused to watch it all.

So brave. I wouldn't be able to if it were me.

When will the Solvers of World Peace be hiring?
There are promising candidates willing to apply. After all, our broken body and jumbled brain are simply inspiring. Brushing our teeth is nothing short of a miracle. Going outside exceeds expectations. My brother's wife is a saint. My husband must have all the patience in the world.

Just how do we do it?
Well, I like to start with breakfast.

NICOLE CHRISTINE CARATAS

Recipe for a Love Potion

Light a candle – two if you have them. Keep Phillippe away or he'll singe his whiskers. Draw the curtains, strike a match, and set the cedarwood incense ablaze. Practise repeating the spell, but only in your mind for now: *ille meus erit*. Take your marble mortar and grind half a sprig of rosemary. Keep your tears from spilling over – those will be added later. Set your pewter cauldron over a fire and bring three cups of jellyfish broth to a boil. Add a toad, followed by two and a half cups of diced toadstool. As you bring it down to a simmer, wipe your tears again – it's still not time. Pluck one leaf from each four-leaf clover in the bunch. Add them to the cauldron one at a time, stirring as you go. Sprinkle in a quarter cup of thorns from red roses. As the potion bubbles, picture the face of your love. Imagine him looking at you, hearts pulsating in his pupils. His arms reaching for you, wrapping around you, pulling you in close. Add the ground rosemary to the cauldron. Think, now, of the love you've lost – is it worth it? Is he worth this?

Remember the promises he made early on. The emphatic way he said he would attend your graduation ceremony; when you warned him it was still months away, he insisted he would be there, holding your hand, cheering you on, no matter when it was. How he swore there was only you, even while he slunk off in the middle of a conversation to surreptitiously message his ex – the same ex you later found out was still listed as his partner on his social media account, though he hid it on his profile. Does the way his curly fringe falls against his eyelashes outweigh the times he didn't call back, the times he missed a date and could only come up with the flimsiest of excuses? Does that little eye crinkle he gets when he smiles make up for his elusive nature, the way he claimed to be yours while keeping his profiles on every dating app live and updated? How often did you pick up his favourite snack for him, drive him to work when he was late, talk him through another grad school spiral, only for him to forget your birthday and your peanut allergy?

You have decided to make a love potion – are you confident in your decision? Is this who you want to be?

As the tears from your broken heart fill your eyes, lean over the steaming cauldron and let them fall in. Salt to taste, and give it a stir. Now, realise this is not what you want. You don't need this. You don't need him. You have you; that's enough.

Extinguish the incense, blow out the candle. Serve your potion in a crystal goblet with a slice of lemon. Drink it down, ignoring the chalky feel on your tongue, and do not utter that spell you memorised. Take these words instead: *meus sum et hoc satis est.*

When the images flash behind your eyelids, accept them. Invite them. They're your wishes after all. A pair of blunt scissors, hacking away at that curling fringe. The crinkle on his face, only now it's between his eyebrows as he frowns. He stands in a crowd, but no one acknowledges him. He's bumped and bounced around, and no one even says sorry. The images speed up now. Him, unable to get a taxi. Him, passed over for every promotion for the rest of his life. Him, losing phone signal on a road trip and getting lost, only to find himself with a flat tire three miles away from the nearest petrol station in the pouring rain. Him, wondering for the rest of his life how he got here, how everything went wrong. You think of him, thinking of you and wondering what would have happened had he given you even an ounce of the respect you deserve. And when you think of him like this, you cannot fight the smile that crosses your lips, or the way the power you now feel sets your body ablaze.

Say those words again, out loud, louder. If your muscles tingle, you've done it right. Find a mirror. Look yourself in the eyes. Do you see those hearts in your pupils? Do you feel it now? Ignore the echo in your ears, the anguish he feels. Forget his whimpers, his tears – you can't be sure they're even real. Take no notice of his change of heart, the way he desperately wishes he could reach you. Do not forgive, but do forget – he's nothing but a blip in your story, a useless side quest, a plot point so minor it wouldn't survive a first edit.

Instead, enjoy your successful potion, the first of many. Go on and love yourself as much as he will hate the rest of his miserable, hexed little life.

ALEX PENLAND

Erasure

An empty suit jacket hung in the air above a pair of black, shining shoes. His heart vanished. His head vanished. His hands vanished. His mouth vanished. He leaned against the bathroom sink and said, *I just don't understand. It's not my fault.* His ribs vanished. He came running through the door. He fumbled with the room key, desperate and out of breath. He fled up the stairs, leaving the party behind him. The guests cried out in alarm. His left lung vanished. His arms vanished. The lobby doors clanged shut behind him. He ran back to the dressing rooms. He left the garden. He told his daughter, *I'll be right back.* He told his daughter, *I hope you know I love you.* His right middle toe vanished. They all stood and left to attend the reception in the hotel garden. The crowd applauded. They both looked beautiful in white. His tear ducts vanished. His daughter walked down the aisle alone. His ring finger vanished. He helped arrange the chairs. They added huge vases full of flowers to the garden walk. The day was overcast and they were afraid of rain. His ears vanished. It was a beautiful old mansion in the country. They drove to the venue in silence. He didn't realize his daughter was listening. *This isn't how it's meant to be*, he told his wife. He still wanted to, despite his misgivings. He was supposed to give her away. The tip of his right index finger vanished. It was his only daughter's wedding day. He woke up in the morning and his hair was gone.

WENDELIN LAW

They are eating the cats!
They are eating the dogs!

I.

Hear me out, townspeople,
they are here, I know, they are

here! Crawling up our walls!
Creeping under our fences!

Lurking among us now!
Beware, my townspeople,

let us stop these creepy crawlers! Yes,
that's what I call them, 'creepy crawlers',

because they shouldn't be here!
This is what we need: another wall!

They are wolves in sheep's clothing,
I kid you not, they are worse! Snakes

in the grass! I'm telling you because
I know a lot more than anyone else!

Townspeople, they are coming!
They are coming here in hordes!

Eating up our food, eating off our welfare!
Soon they'll consume the entire Earth!

And they'll do it very quickly, because
I know the Earth is flat! Listen,

townspeople, they've eaten everything!
They are hanging our pets up on trees

like you'd do a deer for butchering!
They are eating the cats! *Blood is spilling!*

They are eating the doogs! *Oh my god!*
We must build a wall to protect our walls!

We must save our flat Earth from its downfall!
Kill the vermin! How they crawl, they crawl, they crawl!

So they say I'm a demagogue, but listen,
I am not! Because they are eating the cats,

they are eating the dooogs! Townspeople,
listen to me, or they will be eating us all!

II.

The Third World War will come in peace! Perpetual war for perpetual peace! Our last invention: the greatest war machine—the bringer of ultimate peace! We are under the dastardly attack of countless enemies! In all righteousness, we shall live in peace; as for everyone else, may they rest in peace! That's justice, the lawful genocidal feat! Justice, the bombing of the UN's failed Department of Peace! Justice, the autonomous robotic army! Troop by troop and shell by shell, the Third World War will give us all we need! Sing this song of prosperity! Money spewing from the government's truthful mouthpiece! Money spewing from the warlord's arms race charity! Money spewing from the suppurating wounds of mounting dead bodies! Peace, peace! What other contrivance do we need, apart from rail guns, predator drones, and A.G.I. controlled nuclear arsenals? The inevitable triumph of perpetual war—it's peace! There will be no more boundaries! The left is the right and the right is the left! All ideologies will crumble as we meet the judgement of peace! Such lucidity! We are this civilisation from a wet dream, climaxing with mushroom clouds in the name of peace! Come Tsar bombs, come Hydrogen bombs! The nuked sky is raining cats and dogs! The scalding land is cooking them all! The soldiers are eating the cats called humanity! Civilians are eating the dogs called peace! Oh, the Third World Peace! We are eating the cats! We are eating the dogs! Bones stacking up as we are winning absolute victory! Defeat is an impossibility! The Sundial bomb will destroy all our enemies! And nobody on Earth, including us, will live to see what we achieve. When this final bomb receives its command of peace, before we feel it, we will be watching it on live streams. As the reporter's face glitches, the automated voice will annunciate: *Peace! Peace!*

GERRY STEWART

*In My Allotment of Blank Books,
Tea, and Anticipation*

Each summer, I build a scarecrow,
giving her a new Marimekko dress.
I can't be angry when she pierces the pockets
with gorse and my favourite pens.

The rain she cups in her straw hands
blurs any lines I could write,
my rows of metaphors
tipping their onion noses to the clouds.

When the wind wakes the catkins,
bursting their skins,
she offers me a cuppa,
her strawberry tarts studded with snails.

She cannot dissuade the god of hares
from eating my rhubarb
or nibbling on my diaries,
but to be honest
we have both given up trying.

She soothes my scratches
from red ink corrections
with the milk of dandelions.
Torn pages and unwashed spoons
trail in my wake,
a weathervane of my moods,
but only she can read the signs.

She guards my beds of asparagus
and sprouting inspiration
until I swoop like a crow
to feast on the seeds dropped at her feet.

Her summer aches to be written on.
I am digging to pull up the roots
of what I want to say.
All I am grows under her eye.

GERRY STEWART

Marching Away

I prod my children outside,
my coaxing met with whines.
Each grudging step, each refusal
draws the cord taut between us,
close to snapping.
Shouts fade to compromise
as feet drag out the door.

Once in the woods, resistance scatters
in search of a game or adventure,
shrieking with their outdoor voices.

They pick separate routes
over moss, puddles, lichen-draped logs,
to gather scraps growing
and mouldering underfoot.
My children drop away from me
to mushroom, cone, glinting frogs,
white slivers of bark.

Sticks are found and hefted with a crack
against bone-thin pines,
knocking down dead branches.
The echoes build silence
around our earlier harsh words.

I ache with the trees' ghost limbs.
Sap pools, angry and sticking,
fill our breaks.
Wounds heal scarred.
The pines and I continue to feed
our branches that stretch away,
unable to accept the coming loss.

GERRY STEWART

haunted

rain rinses white onto black
reflection exposing my landscape
stone-scratched

each decision
a tumbled cairn
vulnerable to forgiveness

loss returns with the tide
scours me down
to iron and salt

I nurse the etymology of injury
questioning who
has torn down my walls
exposed me to the elements
what words
have weakened my foundations

shelter is found
in the ruins of memory
where I no longer need to throw
the things I love
to the storm
those gathered pearls
moments of loneliness

the night falls monochrome
and sleep still distant
I count the dreams washing in
glints on pebbles

hope is a made thing

WREN TRUE

Picketts

I can't sleep on the journey—more than six hours on a country road where the bumps and divots shake me like a marble in a jar of cream. The trains don't go this far. And the roads are narrow, shimmying between farmland and skinny trees. More like crossing paths for wild animals than roads, I think, not meant for a man pulling a rickshaw.

Fortunately, he doesn't speak much. I think it's my uniform that keeps him to himself, though I always take off my badge when I'm clear of the office.

'I'm sending you out again, Picketts,' the director had said to me at this week's briefing. 'The humble folk respond better to you because you're a woman.'

It's because I take off the stupid badge, I think and will never say.

By late afternoon we arrive at a little town and pass through a market street which is not very busy. The few people waiting for the rickshaw to pass glance warily at its passenger. Down the way, an old man crouches beside a cart of vegetables. A woman shields her baby's face from the sun.

The Necrotic disease has spread slowly. Firstly, it took years for anyone to notice it. Secondly, only when it reached the director's personal circle did he seek answers. And by then it had become commonplace. People were already living with it the same way you live with hog smell—you can try to avoid it, pretend it's not that bad, but it's still there. It gets in your clothes, your home. You sleep with it, eat with it. But the people living out here more than six hours down a country road no longer care about the why and how of this disease. They just want a way to move ahead.

The rickshaw slows along a row of little houses, some with half-sunken roofs and some with weathervanes that squeak in the breeze. I'm not sure which destination is mine. All I have is a list of names, and details about the girl. Her name had been—still is—Pearl. She died at 14. She came back 14 years later.

There are things I've never seen before. Like the image of a farmer's wife standing with an overgrown bramble bush at her back. She's still, like she's getting her photo taken, and somber, like she knows the bush exceeds her in all things: size, beauty, claws. It's so picturesque. It could be a book cover. And I wish for a moment that that was me—that I belonged to the tall grasses and the thistles and wasn't invading them in my uniform.

The rickshaw stops. The driver glances over his shoulder at me, like he's asking what to do next. I wish he'd say something now. I wish I got paid overtime. I scan the names on my list and call over the fence to the brambles: 'Mrs. Wash?'

The farmer's wife moves at last. She bends over to pick something up and then clambers across the yard, flies and grasshoppers leaping out of her way. There's a door on the fence but it's tied with moss-covered rope and she steps over an opening where the slats are broken. She doesn't look at me. The thing she's holding is a pitcher—must be water. She hands it to the rickshaw driver and he drinks.

I'm not used to being greeted last so I jump out of the rickshaw and dust off my uniform. Perhaps a farmer's wife is more straightforward. She needs to look someone in the eye to meet them.

But Mrs. Wash doesn't acknowledge me for what feels like too long. I begin to feel embarrassed for being there at all.

'You can call me ma'am,' says Mrs. Wash finally. 'I have no more husbands.' With this she leaves the pitcher with the driver and walks back toward the house. I scramble for my bags and follow her. The closer I am to the front door, the more I can smell wet laundry, hog fat, and lye. And I can see little hands crawling up the windows. Little eyes staring as I approach.

'The doctor's here,' one of the children screams. I step inside the house and am met with about a dozen little ones looking at me like I've come to collect their ears. They've assembled in a row, straight-backed in crisp, starched outfits.

Mrs. Wash stands between me and them. 'She's not a doctor,' she corrects.

I grind my teeth. 'I'm more like a custodian. I clean up messes.'

One of the children looks at his mother. 'She came all this way to give Pearl a bath?'

'It's not Monday yet,' another one murmurs. Mother silences them all with a look.

I stare at her until she meets my gaze. 'Where is she?' Nobody moves.

Mrs. Wash takes a breath. 'She's from my first marriage. The little ones hadn't even met her before.' Personal details I do not need to know. Shall I repeat myself? The farmer's wife jerks her chin toward the ceiling. 'She's upstairs.'

•

Upstairs is a single room divided by a yellowing curtain. I check both sides to be safe, though I can't tell which is the boys' and which the girls'. I peek under the beds—there are only two—and nobody. There's not much else in terms of furniture. No dressers, no chests. Where do these people store their clothes? Then it occurs to me that no one has been sleeping up here for a while. The children must stay downstairs with their mother every night. They've left behind a pair of dark blue slippers, a worn quilt on one of the beds, and two stuffed toys—a dog and a cow. Cobwebs hang heavy from the corners.

With no sound coming from downstairs, where children and mother wait, it's like the house is holding its breath.

There's scraping by the door. I see a slanted line in the wall. When I crouch in front of it I see it's a wall cabinet. There's no handle, so it's well-hidden. I press against the cabinet door with my fingertips. More scraping from inside. *Found you.*

I use my most honeyed voice, the one that doesn't match the uniform: 'Come on out, little one.'

When the tiny door opens, there's nothing inside—and yet something on the walls and the floor moves like a spider. Right out from under me. Darting across the room and out the window. I think for a moment she's jumped—poor girl! I go to the window and look down. Nothing and nobody. It's all right, I just haven't seen her yet. I search the brambles below, expecting to see a tangle of limbs. Maybe Pearl has run off—maybe it's not the first time.

When I look at the road, I see the rickshaw driver pointing at something. The house. I lean further out the window. Crane my neck. A girl is perfectly balanced with her feet on the iron tongs of the weathervane and she's spinning with it like a top. I can't see her face because all her hair is tangled in front.

When people come back from the grave they are stuck in time. Part of the mystery is why they come back at all when they no longer require nourishment, sleep, or warmth. When they no longer grow. When their families are afraid of them. You would think you'd be glad to be back with your loved ones, back where you left off—but the dead know they're not supposed to be here, not like this. Pearl is trapped in her 14-year-old body with the purple throat that must have killed her. But why is she here? How can Mrs. Wash and her children move ahead when something dead scurries through their home like an independent shadow, and latches on to the closest thing that makes a sound but will not be ashamed of her?

There are things I've never seen. And in my mind the born-again child is still spinning on the weathervane wearing the clothes she was buried in.

HAYLEY BERNIER

everything is the outstretched hand

the air is a knife
gouges portals to past autumns
forlorn and lost
drowning in shadow pressure
when the heart was newly broken
but it felt good when the bruise was pressed
people chatting and being nice
while inside I wondered why
and wished I could have known better
I almost yearn for that ache again
catch myself wishing to be sad
see myself like the fool I am
and shake the shoulders
to clear the etch-a-sketch

know your enemies   (they say)
I think about the time passing
sometimes just a stitch too slow
to fling a hand out to catch

hey there is the leaf falling
its only job fulfilled
terrifying to be so small
amongst the truly vast and tall
the air is sharper
the landscape withers
this is the deep breath in
before the plunge into water

before taking off at a run into the open cold of
    winter's embrace
the sense of hovering uncanny
hesitation but also comfort
but also fear and grief
but also warmth and huddling together
complex roots that dig and prick
it is all so tied up
the chain that holds the cauldron over the fire
bubbling soup full of spells and curses
other cold seasons spent
holing up in my room with my laptop and trash cartoons
so now when I watch rick and morty
pangs for hot chocolate and a hug
for someone to take me seriously
by the fireplace and trust
to share a story that ravels so deep
such a rarity to feel heard

why do I still feel fear
it gets dark out and I feel the sky
fallen heavy blanketing shoulders
go inside   (they whisper)
stay away from the dark
maybe being by the light will feel
                            (what?)

safer steadier realer
it's the sense of feeling not permanent
that I am trying to close the door on
trying to leave behind the curtains and the glass
on the doorstep with the jack-o-lantern
the leaves are already on the sidewalk
I am already 29
and do I still have time

HAYLEY BERNIER

You Do Not Have to Be Good
After Mary Oliver

Standing in the grass
under wet sunlight, the goose
seems to ponder its place.
It stares devotedly forward
as if attending the morning's sermon,
fervent, waiting for the correct call
to allow a burst from stillness
into joyful, confident direction.
But gentle panic slips into its neck
as it curves to allow preening of the wings;
filler conversation,
fidgeting patience.
There is no misinterpreting the mournful tone
as it raises its head high
and blares again its siren.
Pitying humans shake their heads,
summoning teary eyes
at the example of despair in the backyard.
Is it unfortunate to use force for the greater good?
Was it against nature to throw a sheet over the bird,
and press it into a cage in order to free it?
It rattled in the back seat,
as the car drove to the riverbank,
human words of comfort floating
uselessly between them all.
The last seen of the beast was as it emerged
from the small metal door,

straightened its body, and pattered out onto the water,
bobbing for a second
on the harsh current before sprinting towards the sky,
as if just at this moment,
it remembered it could fly.

HAYLEY BERNIER

Ask the River, Ask the Sky, Ask the Person Standing Next to You

I

What do we do without each other
what do we have
to lose here   the ground
receding from us like nervous boundaries
we protect this very line   what do we hold
when the line is moving
away from our markers and borders and maps
when the land protests and goes into hiding

II

water pulled taut
tucks me in

how expansive how powerful
they could so easily pull life from under me
wash it away collapsing
the map into blue

I don't fear the water disappearing
so much as the water disappearing us

III

take nature for granted
sturdy ground beneath
wreaks the havoc
of revenge not aimed at
you

become collateral damage
between thrashing cuts made by humans
and blood seeping from trees
what powerless air to breathe

IV

how do we define progress
darkness so flagrantly wars with the light
each one proclaiming the other's stupidity
like angry sisters fighting over privileges

V

heartache forms our world
grief lies underneath
all of my convictions
fuel to the yearning
burning it makes comfort
sing again
like the whistling of a kettle
like the mewing of a cat
it can be foundational or destructive
it is always both
what do you see now
a new day comes
and are we awake

KATIE HAY-MOLOPO

Aftermath

6. My fingertips fly across the keys. Black and white, crisp lines stacking up on the monitor. I tune out my coworkers. There's no reason for them to change the subject; the weather is bigger than small talk right now. "Did you see? In the last two hours, Milton's gone from a Cat 4 to a Cat 5." "My dad still won't evacuate." "He's right in the pathway." "Storm surge is supposed to be twelve feet." "I know. I can't get him to leave." "How high above sea level?" "Eleven feet." "It's not the wind or tornadoes that get you. It's the water." "We're on the outskirts of it. Won't be that bad." "There will be a lot of water though. And with all the brown water we still have on the ground." "I saw a post from a friend. Says she's still flooded from Helene. 'Everything's already destroyed. What's another flood? Bring it on!' It was kind of a joke, but not really." "It's the same story over and over. We sent this exact email to everyone in our network seven years ago with Irma." "Ocean's only getting hotter. And hurricanes love a good warm bath." "We have to figure out how to communicate this." "We have to figure out how to fix this." "We can't stop it." "We can't look like we're profiting off it either." I inhale, desperate to feel the back of my throat inflate, relax my neck, and let it trickle down my spine.

The sign hanging above our door creaks in the wind. Discreet breaths in and out.

7. We try to speak in code. For the toddlers playing on the mat. We are calm parents. Composed teachers. "Do you think. You know. With the storm." "We're deferring to what the school system says." "I'm just praying it breaks up in the Gulf." "I had someone ask me if I was keeping an eye on it. I said I'm keeping one eye on the storm and two hands at the ready." My daughter starts to sniffle. She's misplaced a green eraser. It's shaped like a book. *Green Eggs and Ham*. "Don't worry, baby. It's at home. Come on. Y'all have a good one." "Be safe!" My palms on the steering wheel. Sticky with age and sweat. Fraying seams in faux leather. The truck in front of me impatiently creeps forward. Cars perpetually queue at the gas station on the corner. I turn up the radio to avoid quiet. Red light, green light, power out, no light.

1. Store number three. We sit for thirty seconds. Unbuckle the girls and find a buggy. Yet another meltdown from inside the trolley. I want to join in but can't burden my husband like that. The climate-controlled air feels too normal. "Did you see the sign on the door?" "Yeah. No electric fans, no coolers, no camp stoves, no propane." "We have propane. I think." "The grills are over there." "I think those are smokers." "We need one with the side burner... You sure we can't just fix the one we have?" "Piping's completely gone." "I just want to boil water." "Did you see the price tag? You must be crazy." "What about charcoal?" "Charcoal could work." "Plenty in stock." "Not many people building campfires to cook pasta, I guess." "Scoot over, baby, I have to put

this next to you." "Mama, I don't want sandwiches for dinner anymore."

2. Waffle House. The same restaurant to which celebrating football players and athletic club boosters and cheerleaders and band members normally flocked on Friday nights in October and they would order waffles and hamburgers and eat and talk loudly and play Journey on the jukebox until 2 am for no reason other than they were young and it was fun—now the gathering place for the bedraggled and exhausted and we fit right in with our unwashed hair and excessive pleasure in eating something cooked by someone else that won't create dishes that will sit in the five-gallon buckets on our porch immersed in water so the ants won't get to them because we're on day I-don't-even-know-what. "Just a waffle please. And sausage. Thanks." I try not to look for too long at the dad who's just walked through the door with a daughter on each hip, pull-ups sporting gangly legs with bare feet and I feel myself relax at the way the cook doesn't even blink, she just says, "Hey hon, there's a free booth right over there, I'll be right over," because he, like us, is no surprise and the base requirement for service here is making it through the door. Another jingle, feet wiping mud on the mat. "Hey Doris, how are you?" "Oh, you know, I'm doing alright." "Is the coffee fresh?" "We can't keep it in the pot, so yeah, it's fresh." I watch my youngest watch the cooks on the line. She makes friends with them all before we leave. My oldest sits in the booth with her half of our waffle, refusing to make friends with anyone. They ask her why she's so sad. I want to say she's not. Just overwhelmed.

5. "I love you, Lord, and I lift my voice to worship You. O my soul, rejoice. Take joy, my King, in what You hear. May it be a sweet, sweet sound in Your ear." My daughter's head is heavy on my chest. I try to relax into the rocking chair, eyes closed though the room is already dark. The fan whirs above us, too quickly—the string is broken. It's out of our control. I feel my chest begin to constrict so I repeat the song and lose myself in her heat and weight and my words soften to sounds enveloping me and her and us. I sit and I rock in the eye of the storm.

3. "Alright, baby, this is the last swing, okay? It's the other little girl's turn." "Oh, don't worry about it. She hates the swing." "How's it been for y'all? Y'all have power?" "Oh, I don't even want to tell you when we got power back." "How come? Y'all get it back early?" "Friday night. Less than a day. And we never lost our water." "Hey, that's awesome! Really. We finally got our power back today. Water too." "Praise God. Oh, watch out for those sticks, honey. Yes, the tree dropped them. Please don't eat them." "I'm sure they'll get around to cleaning this up eventually." "Hardly a priority." "Yeah, we didn't think it'd be this bad." "Oh, we slept through Thursday night like it was nothing." "Hurricane Helene? Just another bad thunderstorm." "Did you see on the news?" "Whole mountainsides wiped clean." "So many people. You know." "Mama, can we go play on the slides now?" And we go, because, why not? They are in their element. Wake, play, eat, sleep, wake, eat, play, eat, sleep. Candlelight and pasta boiled over fire and cold sponge baths and charging our phones in the car to the tune of *Veggie Tales*. It's an adventure.

4. "Our power keeps flickering." "We lost it yesterday for about two hours. We could hear the transformers surging, you know, that *woom* sound." "I had to get off Instagram. Nothing but satellite pictures of walls of clouds and reels of mudslides and stories about houses and people, just, gone." "It's like something out of a movie." "And another on the way." "Like a toddler barreling toward an in-progress game of Jenga." "On top of everything else." "The world just feels fragile." My coworker nods and we sit in silence.

8. Somewhere someone waits on power and potable water and somewhere a Journeyman who just arrived home is called back out into the field and somewhere the tide creeps across someone's kitchen floor and somewhere someone scrolls past these things that are far away and somewhere in the Atlantic a breath of wind becomes a gale that will soon be given a name.

LAURA DE LA PARRA FERNÁNDEZ

For the time being

It's freezing. Our water boiler broke down, and our apartment in Kilburn High Road now has a fist-sized stain spreading across the wallpaper. Litta, my Portuguese flatmate, runs around the house with pots for the leaks. "Not again! Not in the winter! When it's freezing!" she cries. Gianni, our Italian flatmate, watches reality TV unbothered in the living room. After trying to contact our landlord, unsuccessfully, I text Anthony: *Can I come over? Our water boiler broke.* We've been seeing each other for three months, and we still haven't increased the dinner-and-sex-and-maybe-Netflix frequency to more than once a week, sometimes every two weeks. Anthony is quiet, half-French, half-English ("I'm from nowhere," he says, which I know is a cliché, but I like it). He lives across town from me, shares a house with three engineers. The journey from my place to his takes exactly one hour and six minutes if the train doesn't break down. He is developing an app that matches entrepreneurs with investors. But who wants to invest in something that doesn't exist? Maybe that is why neither of us sees a future in our relationship and why it takes a long time for him to text back. He spends all his efforts working hard to get those investors.

And yet, I text him, not knowing what to expect back. The boiler breaking seems like a good excuse to meet. We keep meeting, somehow, though we don't call it dating. It's safer this way. When my ex-boyfriend broke it off via voice text, more than three thousand kilometres away, Litta slapped me in the face and then cooked me a potato stew from her country. "There's no use in crying over a sunken ship," she said. Or something like that. Maybe she was right. At least the stew was delicious. My ex didn't like England, or London, and thought we couldn't keep doing this long-distance thing any longer. It had already been two months since I'd moved here after I got the summer internship. He'd expected I'd change my mind sometime soon, but it wasn't soon enough. And now I couldn't come back. It would be like admitting I had failed.

Three months later, I met Anthony at a pub in Shoreditch. He was the friend of a friend of a friend from a Facebook group of EU expats. We danced. We spoke a mix of English, French, and Spanish. I joked he didn't have to worry about Brexit because he had a British passport, and when he didn't laugh, I secretly hoped he hadn't voted for it. We kissed, and then he disappeared for a while, god knows where. I never asked. That was the first time I thought he wasn't coming back. Then he did, and we went back to mine. "I don't know if we'll see each other again, I'm too busy," he said, matter-of-fact, before asking for my number the next morning. He lived across town, in the south-east of the city. It was a crisp, clear morning when I walked him to Kilburn Station, passing under the bridges to the gate and lightly kissing him goodbye. I went for coffee and a walk in Queen's Park and thought, "Whatever works." I didn't feel sad.

I don't know how I will react when Anthony breaks things off, if he ever does. I assume he'll just stop texting. I'm hoping he'll text back now and that at least this will last through the winter. The summer is okay. I can stretch it. There are always plans to hang out, barbecues in the park, and drinks by the canal. Everyone always remembers why they moved to London in the summer. Though it's easy to forget it in the winter when sleep becomes gloomy and heavy like smog.

With my ex, I thought it was my fault. I somehow always make people mad at me. It's like when I'm working in the library and I can never quite spell things correctly: people get upset, restless at having to deal with the foreign clerk. Well, it's not my dream job, but I like it. I never imagined I could get paid for searching and setting books out. I like the order. I like the quiet. I like having some spare time to read. Most of all, I like it when they order something from the cold, dark storage room. The light above the clerk desk plunges me into a state of drowsiness, as if my short-sightedness increased throughout the day. When I go down to the storage room, I close my eyes and lean my forehead against one of the metal shelves until the pressure fades away.

There's so much I can't afford in this city – I can't afford a new boiler, a queen-sized bed, or to live by myself. I can't afford fancy dinners or Uber rides on the weekends. Yet I can be anywhere, anytime, and nobody asks where I am. Ever since living here, I have taken to long walks everywhere. I want to soak up this city. Outside of my working hours, I have nowhere to go, nowhere else to be at a specific time. If it's not raining, I like going up to Parliament Hill, sitting on a bench and looking at the skyline for hours. Parks in this city always get quiet before it's dark, except when it's warm. Afterwards, I wander about the streets of Hampstead, peering into the uncurtained windows of beautiful, expensive-looking houses I'll never be able to afford. I like to watch people going about their daily business, eating dinner, putting their children to bed, watching TV on their own. I am good at not being noticed.

Observing strangers makes me realize that I am completely alone, and that fills me with joy and dread. Nobody knows where I am at this time. "If you go, you'll forget who you are," my ex said, when he was not yet my ex. "You've changed," he said the first time he came to visit. "You can come home any time," my father tells me, hoping I will go back. I don't think I had changed. I don't know if I want to go back. For the first time, I don't want to plan anything. I know Litta sounds different when I listen to her speak Portuguese instead of English. Does my Spanish sound different now, too? "I never thought about it," Anthony said when I asked him. I asked him why he'd moved to London. "Why not?" he said. "I feel like anything could happen here." I liked his answer. I liked his smell, too, and I wanted to soak it up while it lasted.

I'm helping Litta boil water to shower when I receive a text. It's probably our landlord, who lives out of town. But I'm proven wrong again. "Sure," the text reads, "I'll be at home by ten. I can grab some Vietnamese on the way." I sigh with relief. At least, for the time being, we get one more night.

CARLY CRAIG

Last Snow in Athens

The night guard has started singing to the statues. In the early hours, his voice is threadbare; it's a paltry offering to a stone-faced audience, but it's what he has. Three months in, the silence has become unbearable. He walks among the stelae through these tomb-like, windowless halls and feels the stifling weight of time collapsing. Once, living hands threw pottery, forged precious metals, chiseled stone—all so that these objects may have a life in the world: so the people may be fed, and the gods may be worshipped, and the dead may be remembered. The work begs to be witnessed. But the doors are long closed now, and instead of the awestruck public, the work has only Nikos: thirty-six, father of one, owner of a reedy singing voice and a nervous tic in his left hand, renter of an apartment in Neos Kosmos.

At the beginning of his secondment, when he was perpetually exhausted and missing Seb and Kleio, Nikos often contemplated the last time the National Archaeological Museum remained closed for so long. It was the winter of 1940, and war was on its way to Athens. To protect their collection from Nazi bombing and looting, the museum staff turned history on its head. They pried up the flagstones and dug deep trenches below the museum floors. They returned their relics to the ground, cast in plaster, coated in wax, boxed in crates, bound in fabric. When they were done, they restored every tile to its rightful place, polished the floors clean, and vowed to keep the museum's secrets, no matter the cost. They prayed that the strata of sand and concrete would once again carry their history safely into an uncertain future.

Axis troops invaded Athens in April 1941. 'Have courage and patience,' Athens Radio urged their fellow citizens in the final hours before the city fell. 'Prove yourselves worthy of your history...Greece will live again.' German soldiers pushed straight to the Acropolis, where they raised the Nazi flag. But when they went to plunder the National Museum, they were thwarted. They found its echoing halls empty—miraculously unoccupied.

Nikos must have repeated those facts to guests on his tours thousands of times over the years. The defiant trickery of his forbearers seemed almost mythic. It made him proud to be Greek, proud to work in this monumental place preserved by the tenacity of ordinary employees like him. Now, the present complicates the past, and he finds himself dwelling on different details. How did it feel to watch the enemy marching toward Athens, knowing their only recourse was to hide their beloved charges and hope they would not be found? How did it feel to exist in the untold middle of their story, under indefinite Nazi occupation? Is the narrative he leans on for courage only powerful because he knows how it ends?

After all, here's history knocking on his own door, and Nikos has never felt so impotent. It's not just patrolling a closed museum. It's slipping past Kleio, sleeping odd hours in a half-empty bed, pacing around their tiny apartment pretending not to worry as Seb's eyes go duller with each day spent slumped over a tablet in that same corner, barely tuned in to his online classes. Their boy is wilting. Their sweet, social kid, so silent and still. A primal horror: this slow petrification is killing him. Just a few days ago, the government announced that the rules would tighten again and schools would close only twelve days after reopening. When he heard the news, fear struck Nikos with fresh violence. Cases are up. The death toll is rapidly surpassing other countries in Europe. Nikos would go to war to save his son, but how do you resist an enemy so intangible as a virus? How do you endure its occupation?

He is heading back toward the exit now, his shift nearly finished, but he makes a point of pausing in the red-painted room housing the Jockey of Artemision, one of his favorite statues in the collection. This life-sized horse gallops forward in frantic, beautifully rendered motion. Atop his back is a small boy, chiton flying in the wind, hand outstretched to hold reins that corroded away in the two thousand years this pair spent resting on the Aegean seabed. The work is extraordinary, Nikos always stressed to visitors, not just for its artistry but for its improbability. Most ancient Greek bronzes like this one have not survived; over centuries, their material was reclaimed and reforged for new purposes. How strange, then, that a shipwreck saved this horse and his rider, and so they gallop on.

He makes a mental note to tell Seb that story later. That and the war stuff—shipwrecks and Nazis and buried treasure will hold the boy's attention for a little while, at least. They can pretend their apartment is set in a bubble on the seafloor, their own city of Atlantis, and perhaps when the divers find them and haul them up again someday, the world will be completely changed.

Heartened by this image, Nikos fishes a crumpled mask out of his pocket and puts it on, pinching the aluminum tab across the bridge of his nose. He moves briskly through the remaining rooms and into the entrance hall, stopping short of the tape on the floor marking two meters from the front desk. There, Panagiotis sits tapping away at his phone, ignoring the static gray security footage playing on the monitors.

"Where's Christos?" Nikos asks the older man.

"Late." Panagiotis looks up, bleary-eyed. "Haven't you heard? There's a freak snowstorm out there. The buses aren't running."

"Snow?" Nikos glances toward the heavy wooden doors, a glimmer of excitement stirring in his chest.

"Lots. Will you be able to get back okay?"

"Yeah, sure." He drifts toward the cloakroom. "Hey, do you need me to stay until—"

"No, get home to your boy." The crow's feet around his colleague's eyes crinkle.

Nikos pats a hand on his heart twice and grins at Panagiotis under his mask before hurrying off to fetch his things.

When he steps through the front doors a few moments later, the plaza is unrecognizable, blanketed under at least half a meter of snow. The trees droop, limbs made heavy by the accumulation of thick, fluffy flakes still drifting through the air. The scene is marvelous—more reminiscent of Nikos's childhood visits to the mountains than anything he's seen in Athens before. His eyes water with cold and pure astonishment.

He's halfway down the marble steps out front, moving gingerly to avoid a slip and fall, when it occurs to him that his moped isn't going anywhere in this weather. Briefly, he considers the Metro, but as he rips his mask off, giving his lungs a full hit of the sharp, wintry air, glee overtakes reason, and he decides that he's walking.

Patision Avenue is just beginning to wake up. Few cars have dared venture out onto the roads, but Nikos sees a delivery van crawling along the wide thoroughfare, high beams ablaze in the early morning half-light. One shopkeeper watches from his doorway with a bewildered smile on his face while another wades through the drifts to help direct the van into place. Two determined joggers forge on through the snow in perfect step with one another, until one's foot slides out from under her, and she has to grab the other's arm to keep upright. The two women break into a musical fit of laughter. Lights blink on. Children press their noses to icy windows that fog with their hot, sleepy breath. In the dark of the night, something magical has happened. Their city is transformed.

By the time Nikos reaches Monasteraki Square, where modern buildings give way to the ancient heart of Athens, more people are out in the streets, bundled up in their warmest clothes, masks on, glasses steamy. They move as if in a daze, repeatedly turning their faces to the sky in wonder. The clouds are the same pale gray as the stone buildings. The snow piles thicker yet on every available surface. It's a dreamy wash of a landscape, and there, above it all, the tall mound of the Acropolis starts to come into view, the Parthenon ghost-like in the wintry haze.

Drawn in that direction, Nikos continues up the hill past the sprawling ruins of Hadrian's Library. The path is steep and slippery here, and his boots squelch from snow melting down his ankles, but he barely notices. He traipses on through the narrow streets of Plaka, where the monochrome landscape shatters into pinks and yellows and greens, brightly plastered buildings, warmly lit, cozy in spite of the storm. On, down the flank of the hill, toward the often congested Kallirrois, now devoid of cars. A family runs along the road, pulling a toddler on a toboggan and kicking up snow for a playful collie. Nikos is racking his brain as to what in their apartment can be repurposed as a sled when he hears a merciful sound: a group of boys, a few years older than Seb, in peals of gleeful laughter as they run and dodge between trees, pelting snow at one another.

Ahead, two young police officers turn a corner. One elbows the other and points at the children. Please, Nikos thinks, just let them have this. Before he can decide whether to intercede, he sees the officers crouch down to gather their own handfuls of snow. A reprieve, a gift.

His heart pounds with happy exertion. His cheeks glow. It's not far now, just round the corner into Neos Kosmos, down his street, and there it is. Three floors up, a light shines through their kitchen blinds. Kleio, awake. He pauses for a moment, staring up at their balcony, a soft smile on his face. He imagines it through her eyes: waking up, brewing a bleary coffee, finding her glasses. He fires off a quick text and sets to work trampling a large heart shape into the fresh powder on their street.

"Hey, Romeo!" a voice calls down from their balcony a few moments later. "Are you coming upstairs, or what?"

Kleio leans over the railing, coffee in hand, snowflakes catching in her dark hair. Nikos shields his eyes and grins up at her, soaked through and utterly delighted with himself. She shakes her head at him. He thinks her smile might be warm enough to melt all the snow in Athens.

Inside, he sheds his layers and peppers her cheeks with frozen kisses before fetching a handful of snow from the balcony to go and wake their son. In the dark cave of Seb's bedroom, the boy lies asleep on his back, calm, still, orderly, the antithesis of his waking self. Nikos sits for a moment by his bedside and takes in his son's peaceful face and the slow rise and fall of his breathing. So beautiful. Maybe the most beautiful thing Nikos has ever seen. Softly, he begins to sing: *My bright little moon, light my way...* And Sebastian does what the statues cannot: he stirs and opens his warm brown eyes.

In 1946, when the war was over and the occupiers were gone, employees took pickaxes to the National Archaeological Museum floors. There, in the grand halls of this nineteenth-century temple to the art of their ancestors, they conducted an incongruous, full-scale excavation. They dug through the strata of sand and concrete. They unwrapped fabric, peeled away wax, broke open crates, and lifted the largest statues in their collection back into the light. Nike of Epidaurus. Poseidon of Melos. The Jockey of Artemision. They were never far away. 'It was,' the poet Giorgos Seferis would write, 'a resurrection dance of rising figures, a Day of Reckoning of bodies that filled you with mad joy.' In 1947, the museum reopened its doors to the public.

Nikos shows wide-eyed Seb the shimmering, white snowball he has brought in from the balcony. "Hey, bright little moon," he says. "Wake up. It's time to go outside."

CONTRIBUTORS

HAYLEY BERNIER (she/her) is a queer writer and editor from Canada. Hayley writes poetry, but is also trying really really hard to draft a novel. She aspires to be a published writer and editor, but given the job economy, she would also do any job involving animals. She loves sushi, reading by the fireplace channel, and cackling with friends. You can follow her sporadic posts @burnyayhayley on Instagram.

NICOLE CHRISTINE CARATAS (she/her) is a Pushcart-nominated writer and editor living in Edinburgh. She holds a PhD in creative writing from the University of Edinburgh and has been published in the UK and abroad. Her speciality is historical fiction, and she is currently working on her second novel. When she isn't writing, she can be found curled up with a book and her cat, Finn. Find her on Instagram: @_nicolesbooknook

THOMAS CARROLL lives and writes in Edinburgh, having moved to the city almost ten years ago for his studies. His main interest is in speculative fiction, writing short stories and novels that try to explore the effects of contemporary issues through a different lens.

CARLY CRAIG is a graduate of the New England Young Writers' Conference and the University of Edinburgh, where she was awarded an MA in English literature. Her short stories have been published in *Jambalaya Magazine*; *Little Fish, Big Bait*; and *Hillfire Anthology*.

EMERSON ROSE CRAIG is an internationally published author of fantastical and strange short fiction. She holds an

MSc in creative writing from the University of Edinburgh. When not writing, she works as a contributing editor at *The Selkie* and on the editorial collective for *CALYX Press*. Find her on socials: @emersonrosecraig

LAURA DE LA PARRA FERNÁNDEZ teaches American literature in Madrid. She has authored a novel, a short story collection, and three poetry collections, all published in Spain under her pen name Emily Roberts. She obtained her MSc in creative writing at the University of Edinburgh, and has lived in different places across Europe and the US. Find her on Instagram: @emyliroberts

JULIA GUILLERMINA lived in Edinburgh at some point; it was a very literary experience – the black walls of old churches with their crooked tombstones, meeting so many writers from across the world... Now she can borrow from this experience while teaching history and geography to Parisian teenagers. Instagram @julia.gui_

KATIE HAY-MOLOPO is:
1) a believer in Jesus, constantly seeking firm ground, quiet spaces, and hope.
2) the mother of two beautiful girls deeply loved by both her and her husband.
3) doing her best to pursue her writerly dreams *and* fulfill the obligations of adulthood.
4) online at LetsBeHuman.Substack.com.

MIRIAM HUXLEY (she/her) is an award-winning writer and editor from British Columbia. She holds a PhD in creative writing from the University of Edinburgh. She has been published in *The London Reader*, *From Arthur's Seat*, *HARTS & Minds*, and *Louden Singletree*. Her other interests involve meeting cats, researching the best vegan mac and cheese, and drinking a lot of oat lattes. She is currently working on a novel about dangerous plants. Find her on socials @miriamhuxley and miriamhuxley.substack.com

M.H. MONICA fell in love with books at age three. With a master's degree in creative writing from the University of Edinburgh, she has edited and published over 200 picture books and now creates comics and webtoons fulltime with *Toonsutra*. When she's not immersed in fiction, you can find her playing with her dog or dreaming up her next adventure!

ALEX PENLAND is a former Smithsonian kid. They spent their childhood running rampant through an early career as a child adventurer. Now a Pushcart-nominated author, Alex lives in Scotland while studying for a PhD. Their work has been internationally published; *Andrion* is their first novella. Catch them on most social media as @alexpenname and on their website, AlexPenland.com

MALINA SHAMSUDIN (she/her) identifies as a storyteller. Her grown-up stories took to print via journalism, then public relations for an agency, multinational, and now, a non-profit. When not on the hunt for the perfect flat white, this Malaysian can be found grazing on crafty reality TV, talking to dogs, or browsing the children's section of a bookstore. Her other Dark Forest fairy tale retellings can be found in *From Arthur's Seat Volume 7*, *Silly Goose Volume 1* and *Hillfire Anthology*, volumes 2-3.

TESS SIMPSON is a children's bookseller and writer living in Edinburgh, where she can often be found yelling about the importance of children's fiction, graphic novels and translated picture books. She writes about magic and childhood and monsters, and is currently finishing her first novel.

GERRY STEWART is a poet, teacher, and editor in Finland. *Post-Holiday Blues* was published by Flambard Press, UK. Her poetry is widely published and appeared in *The Poetry Archive*'s World View, *iamb poetry* and the *Eat the Storms* poetry podcast. Her blog can be found at thistlewren.blogspot.fi

WREN TRUE is a fiction writer from Des Moines, Iowa. She likes pointing at animals and taking two-hour naps. She also has a Substack now: wrentrue.substack.com

RUBY VALLIS lives in Bristol. She writes short stories, and when she doesn't, she edits (for the third time) a novel set in Colombia, where she was born. Her short stories are inspired by both Colombian and British culture. One of her short stories was published in 2018, in *Voices Along the Road Anthology*, in aid of child refugees.

As a writer, editor, and human, HANNA-MARIA VESTER is forever playing hide and seek with what feels thrilling, fulfilling, and true. It's not always pretty. But it's usually at least a little bit funny. Ya gotta, ya know? Read her writing in *Hillfire Anthology*, volumes 1-4, and *Silly Goose Volume 2*!

WESTER WAGENAAR writes quirky short stories in Dutch and English. He holds a master's degree in creative writing from the University of Edinburgh, and his writing has appeared in publications including *From Arthur's Seat*, *Gutter Magazine*, and *Lezenswaardig!*. When not putting pen to paper or saving society as a civil servant, Wester enjoys (board) games, heavy music, and exploring cities in search of the cutest cats.

ALEXIA WDOWSKI lives in a small town by the sea where she is the manager of an independent bookshop. She writes about outsiders, risk-takers, wilderness, books, and the surreal qualities of daily life. She is currently working on completing a novel. You can find more of her writing here: www.alexiawdowski.co.uk

HILLFIRE MEMBER FEATURE

WENDELIN LAW is a writer from Hong Kong. She is the co-winner of the 2024 Edwin Morgan Poetry Award. She is currently working on her first poetry collection, *Whaling*, which is commended by the 2024 James Berry Poetry Prize. Her debut pamphlet, *as wild as*, is upcoming.

Wendelin Law on being part of Hillfire Press:

When I started submitting poems to literary magazines, I realised quickly it was going to be a lonely process full of rejections. I didn't want to give up, because I'd only just begun, but there were also conflicting thoughts, e.g., what if I was wasting my time; how long should I persist?

Just as I wondered if this was going to continue forever, Lena (founder and editor-in-chief) invited me to contribute to Hillfire Anthology Volume 1.

Hillfire is a very important community to me.

Instead of formulaic, unexplained rejections, we work together in groups and multiple editing rounds to get everybody's work published in the anthology.

There's nothing better than writerly support and discussions.

Because of the editing rounds, I get to analyse different pieces of writing in a new light, and this process also elevated my poems, some of which would otherwise have been scrapped.

The Hillfire editing process is a fulfilling path of rediscovery and poet self-love. I learned to re-evaluate 'effective' and 'ineffective' elements in my work. It is often to question what I thought of as 'effective' and, counterintuitively, to put faith and lots of work on what appeared to be 'ineffective' but is actually full of potential (e.g., overly abstract imagery, a run-on line, or an illogical expression that speaks of a powerful emotion). This is one of the instances that makes the comments and discussions in editing rounds helpful and invaluable.

Working together to produce this anthology which thrives on support, I reclaimed my words, once buried by doubts, now resounding in clarity. I'm incredibly proud to be part of Hillfire, and especially so in turbulent times—we need independent publication communities where we can speak truly and firmly of ourselves.

If you would like to support us supporting writers like Wendelin, you can donate to Hillfire Press here:

Or find us at Hillfirepress.com

www.ingramcontent.com/pod-product-compliance
Lightning Source LLC
Chambersburg PA
CBHW020538080526
44583CB00013B/904